Men's Gymnastics Coaching Manual

MEN'S GYMNASTICS COACHING MANUAL

Lloyd Readhead

CROWOOD

First published in 1987 by
Springfield Books Limited
Norman Road, Denby Dale
Huddersfield, West Yorkshire HD8 8TH

This edition published in 1997 by
The Crowood Press Ltd
Ramsbury, Marlborough
Wiltshire SN8 2HR

British Library Cataloguing-in-Publication Data
A catalogue record for this book is available from the
British Library.

ISBN 1 86126 076 8

Picture Credits
Illustrations: Bill Barden.

Printed and bound in Great Britain

Contents

Preface vi

Foreword by John Atkinson vii

Acknowledgements viii

Section	Topic	page
1.0	The gymnastics coach	1
2.0	Insurance	2
3.0	The provision and maintenance of a gymnastics facility	3
4.0	General safety in gymnastics	4
5.0	First aid and emergency provision	10
6.0	Caring for the injured gymnast	11
7.0	Class management	15
8.0	Planning the training	21
9.0	Mechanical principles	23
10.0	Anatomy and physiology	38
11.0	The pre-session warm-up	49
12.0	Physical preparation and conditioning	51
13.0	Body and spatial awareness	85
14.0	The trampoline and rebound as aids to teaching	91
15.0	The teaching of gymnastics elements	99
16.0	Floor elements	99
17.0	Side horse – pommel horse	113
18.0	Rings	126
19.0	Vaulting	145
20.0	Parallel bars	156
21.0	Horizontal bar exercises	176
22.0	Choice of apparatus	197
23.0	Select bibliography	200

Preface

The aim of this coaching manual is to provide a resource of information for coaches embarking upon a gymnastics coaching career. The manual is designed to meet the needs of the developing coach and is therefore closely related to the BAGA Men's Coaching Awards Syllabus.

Gymnastics activities are very complex and it is necessary for a coach to have a good understanding of a number of disciplines. The coach's knowledge must therefore encompass such aspects as teaching methods, anatomy, physiology, psychology, biomechanical principles, planning, programming, character development, etc. The level of understanding in each discipline will vary according to the level of coaching; this manual has particular relevance to the BAGA Men's Grade 4 Coaching Syllabus and will be of value to both coaches and course tutors. It is intended that the content of the manual is used as a coaching course resource pack and each course candidate is advised to obtain a copy prior to attending the course. The manual will also serve as a constant source of reference for the conscientious and caring gymnastics coach.

Gymnastics 'styles' and gymnastics 'techniques' are in a state of constant change and there is invariably more than one way to perform or teach a particular skill. This is part of the intriguing and complex nature of the sport of gymnastics. The information in this manual is based upon sound, proven techniques and should prove to be a thorough basis upon which the foundation for safe, effective coaching can be laid.

Lloyd Readhead
National Coach (Men's Coaching)

Foreword *by John Atkinson*

The need for this manual has long been recognised, and I know of no-one better qualified – schoolboy enthusiast to British International, club coach to National Coach – to write it. Lloyd Readhead has created internationals from raw aspirants and inspired and guided young people to become excellent coaches. He has administered and administrated; Chairman of his Regional Schools Association, member of the BAGA Men's Technical Committee and Chairman of its Coaching Panel. A person who *gives* so much is bound to *receive* – what Lloyd 'received' was a wealth of experience and knowledge relevant to every aspect of men's gymnastics. Once again in producing this book he has 'given': the time, effort and research necessary to create such a valuable work must have been taken from his sleeping hours, for he has maintained his invaluable contribution to British gymnastics whilst writing it.

He has analysed 'what' is required to achieve success in gymnastics coaching and performance and 'how' it can be achieved. Too often authors in this field have paid too much attention to 'what' and almost forgotten the 'how'. He has also structured the contents so that the coach understands the essentiality of establishing the correct physical profile, as well as the importance of co-ordination, balance and the aesthetic qualities necessary in gymnastics performances, thus ensuring the effective part this manual will play in all coach education in men's gymnastics in the future. It will provide the background for excellent teaching and coaching.

A coach needs to have 'the eye' – the perceptive qualities of the bird of prey linked with the abilities to 'freeze frame' and then 'play back in slow motion'. Once this visual process has taken place and the necessary analysis been made, the coach must give the right advice, couched in readily understandable terms, to eradicate the exposed error and increase the perfection of the performance. Those areas of the book concerned with biomechanical analysis and skill assessment will help the reader to achieve such qualities of observation.

The illustrations really complement the text. Bill Barden has done an excellent job in maintaining technical accuracy whilst producing the necessary artistic effect.

Lloyd Readhead has successfully managed and coached British gymnasts in many countries, at World and European Championship standard. He has received recognition of his talent for coach education from the International Olympic Committee and the International Federation of Gymnastics. His ability to communicate at all levels is evidenced in this most valuable and technically worthwhile gymnastics manual.

John Atkinson
Technical Director
British Amateur Gymnastics Association

Acknowledgements

The compilation of a gymnastics coaching manual is an enormous task and one which cannot be undertaken without the support of many people and an abundance of reference material. My gratitude is extended to the many friends, colleagues and acquaintances who have helped and influenced me during my own development as a coach. Without that help I should not have had the armouring to attempt the seemingly endless task of compiling this manual.

Special thanks are due to the following for their support and inspiration: my colleagues in the BAGA Technical Department, both coaching and administrative staff; the Men's Technical Committee of the BAGA; the BAGA Men's Coaching Panel Members; Dr Craig Sharpe (anatomy and physiology), Dr Lew Hardy (psychology) and John Newton (mechanics) for their advice in compiling the contents of the Men's Coaching Syllabus. My gratitude is also extended to Bill Barden, who applied his immense artistic talents to the illustrations.

I am pleased to present this manual and trust that it will be of value in the continued development of our sport and its participants.

Lloyd Readhead
National Coach (Men's Coaching)

1.0 The gymnastics coach

1.1 The role of the coach

A coach must play many parts in his role as coach. To his performers and fellow coaches he must become:

Teacher: imparting knowledge and skills.
Motivator: inspiring and encouraging his students to achieve higher standards.
Trainer: ensuring good physical preparation and awareness.
Psychologist: offering advice, listening to problems and ensuring that the performer is mentally prepared for the task in hand.
Disciplinarian: ensuring that the performer relates to those personal behavioural standards appropriate to the sport of gymnastics.
Scientists: keeping abreast of new developments, analysing performance, evaluating results and advising on technique.
Manager: organising and planning training, obtaining good training facilities, establishing public relations.
Friend: listening, advising and supporting the performer through childhood, puberty, maturation, courtship, marriage and parenthood.

These are but a few of the many roles a coach must play and a successful coach will be one who is a committed and caring person.

A coach must form a personal philosophy and be prepared to amend that philosophy upon discussions and advice from other possibly more experienced coaches. This philosophy must be based upon his beliefs, his commitments, the time he can offer to his performers, and the necessary traits within the sports.

It is good advice to all coaches frequently to examine their own personal motivation and to ensure that they are not exploiting the talents of their performers merely to satisfy their own personal ego.

1.2 The legal responsibility of the coach

The coach must accept full *Loco Parentis* responsibility for the pupils whilst in his care and must be concerned with the following:
a.   The coach must care for the health and safety of each participant.
b.   The coach must have the competence for the role he or she is performing.
c.   The coach must be fully qualified to do that which he or she has undertaken.
d.   The coach must perform in a reasonable, prudent and professional manner.

1.3   The prudent and caring coach

The prudent and caring coach will ensure that the following principles are implemented and continually upheld:

a.   A safe environment is provided at all times.
b.   Clear and adequate instructions are given prior to permitting a performance.
c.   Coaching methods and procedure are continually assessed for the safety of both performer and coach (handler).
d.   Only competent persons are permitted to supervise or coach an activity or element.
e.   The clothing and special equipment (ie. handguards) to be worn by the performer is suitable, is not loose fitting, and is in good order.
f.   The health status of each performer should be known.
g.   Medical advice should be sought in case of injury and only immediate first aid should be administered by persons who are not medically qualified.
h.   An accurate record of injuries and ensuing actions should be kept.
i.   Medical approval should be sought following a serious injury before permitting a performer to recommence training.
j.   The coach is immediately accessible and never leaves the premises while a session is in progress.
k.   A well-publicised safety procedure and first aid policy is implemented and adhered to.

2.0 Insurance

2.1   The need for insurance cover

Adequate insurance cover is essential for all persons involved in coaching and should protect the coach against undue financial loss if a case of negligence is found in the event of an accident. Types of insurance available include:

a.   *Liability insurance:* Compensation is made available to the injured person when negligence on the part of the coach is proven.

b.   *Accident insurance:* Compensation is made available to the injured person because an accident has occurred and not because negligence on the part of the coach has been proven.

c.   *Third party civil liability:* Compensation may apply to a participant injuring a coach, or fellow participant, spectator or official. It may also apply to an event organiser, a club, an association, a facility owner or a sports equipment firm.

It is recommended that all personnel involved in gymnastics should consult the BAGA Head Office for details concerning their membership and insurance scheme or consult an insurance company or broker to discuss insurance cover schemes. It is also advisable that, when arranging transportation of teams or individuals to events, checks are made to ensure that all drivers and vehicles have adequate cover.

2.2   Parental permission or waiver forms

These should give consent for the participant to take part in stated activities at local or away venues and permission for the application of emergency medical care as the need arises.

The consent forms should have an agreement not to hold the club or coach responsible for any injury occurring during the stated activities or travel to an event.

The consent or waiver forms ought to be introduced to all participants, but it should be remembered that:

a.   They basically indicate that the parents acknowledge in writing that they rightfully assume the risks normal to the activity.
b.   They *do not* give licence to those conducting the activity to be negligent.
c.   An adult *cannot* sign away the rights of a minor.

3.0   The provision and maintenance of a gymnastics facility

It is incumbent upon all coaches to ensure that a safe environment is provided at all times. It is therefore necessary to ensure that frequent checks are carried out to ensure the safety of the following.

3.1   The facility

This is basically the responsibility of the owner of the facility but a coach should frequently check and report any defects or faults in areas such as: the condition of the building; access to the building; fixtures and fittings in the gymnasium; lighting; heating; floor surfaces; changing and shower areas; and that storerooms are safe and tidy.

3.2   The equipment

It is the responsibility of all coaches frequently to examine and report on the safe condition of the gymnastics apparatus and never to permit faulty equipment to be used. The inspection should include the condition and maintenance of: floor plates, shackles, butts, support fittings, chains, spring boards, bars (watch for splintering), and matting (take care that it is not torn or damaged).

3.3   First aid provision

Frequent checks should be made on the provision of adequate first aid equipment and supplies (please refer to Section 5 on First Aid).

4.0   General safety in gymnastics

It is essential that precautions are taken at all times during gymnastics activity to ensure a safe environment. The following recommendations should be supplemented with other aspects of safety as suggested throughout this book (1.2; 1.3; 3.0).

4.1   Preparation of the gymnast

Before attempting to perform a gymnastics movement it is imperative that the gymnast has been fully prepared both mentally and physically. It is therefore recommended that the following guidelines are implemented.

a.   The physical abilities of the gymnast must be suitably developed to perform the movement. Appropriate strength, flexibility and body awareness must be developed.
b.   Carefully select progressive sub-skills which relate to the complete skill and ensure that the gymnast has complete mastery of all stages before progressing.
c.   Use a visual aid to enhance motor skill learning. This could be in the form of a demonstrator, video, snapgraph pictures, film or picture. The use of the visual aid will enable the gymnast mentally to visualise the skill and will increase his confidence and motivation towards learning the skill.
d.   Ensure that the gymnast is motivated to perform the skill and that there are no anxieties or fears which may cause an abortive attempt.
e.   Both the gymnast and coach (spotter) should be fully conversant with the mechanics of the skill and aware of the method of 'handling' to be offered by the coach.

4.2   Competent spotting

'Spotting' is essential to the safe learning of gymnastic skills and involves the techniques of observation and handling to ensure the safe performance of the skill.

Good spotting will guide the 'shape or pattern' of movement, reinforcing the timing and rhythm, and minimise the risk of falls or mistakes.

The performer must have complete trust and confidence in the 'spotter' if he or she is to approach the skill without undue anxiety. This trust will be assured through the following:

a.   The spotter must be fully conversant with all aspects of the skill. This will involve a mechanical understanding and a thorough knowledge of the progressive skills.

b.   The spotter must be alert to any signs of anxiety or errors in performance by the gymnast.
c.   The spotter must offer clear and precise instructions and ensure that the gymnast understands the instructions.
d.   The spotter must have adequate experience in spotting or handling.
e.   The spotting technique must ensure the safety of the gymnast.

4.3   Structuring a support technique

There are four common methods adopted in spotting: handspotting; handheld belt; overhead belt; and overhead travelling rig and belt. The choice of method will be greatly influenced by the skill to be performed in respect of distance travelled, degree of flight, involvement of twisting elements etc. Further advice on the selection will be available in the sections concerning the teaching of the various skills. When designing a spotting technique, the following points should be considered:

a.   Design an apparatus set-up which is adjusted in height and width to suit the individual gymnast and provide a suitable protective padding which will not inhibit the performer but will safeguard against a fall.
b.   Study the skill and select a handling technique which will assist in the shaping of the performance and not hamper the gymnast.
c.   The spotter must be in a position to be close enough to the performer to guide and catch him in the event of a failed attempt at the skill.
d.   Consider the points at which the gymnast is most at risk through possible collapse or loss of grip and design the support technique to give assistance at these points.
e.   The spotter must have good access to move in quickly to catch the performer in order to prevent a fall.
f.   When using handbelts and overhead rigs ensure that there is no risk of entanglement between the belt, rig, apparatus, gymnast or coach. Also, check that the correct number of turns or wraps in the belt have been used prior to each attempt at the skill. This is particularly important when performing skills which involve twists or movements from giant swings.
g.   As the performer's confidence in the skill improves, the degree of assistance will be reduced, but it is essential that any modification to the handling technique still permits adequate support to be provided in the event of a failed attempt. Any adjustments to the support technique should not cause anxiety to the gymnast.

The degree of success of a performance is largely dependent upon the initial phase of the skill. If the 'timer' aspect or 'set-up' is incorrect the gymnast must modify the remainder of the skill and a less effective performance will result. The spotter should be aware of this point and should provide assistance to ensure that at each attempt the initial phase is reproduced consistently.

4.4   Teaching recovery and landing from falls

Correct landing technique and the ability to recover from falls are essential to the safety of the gymnast and these fundamental skills should be taught during the initial preparatory training of a young gymnast. The development of these skills will be dealt with under section 13.2 and it is desirable that coaches and gymnasts are aware of the importance of these skills.

4.5   Avoiding injury due to overtraining

To consolidate the performance of a skill it is necessary to perform the skill many times. However, to repeat a movement requires a *degree of endurance* and coaches should be aware that it is likely that *fatigue will occur* during a session. This is particularly likely with young gymnasts and the *onset of fatigue* results in loss of co-ordination and the risk of failure and falling is increased. Coaches must recognise this factor and terminate the workout accordingly.

This lack of endurance, resulting in fatigue, is the cause of many failures and falls during the dismount at the end of a demanding gymnastics routine. It is therefore good practice to ensure that once the skill itself is perfected it is then progressed by frequent repetitions involving the execution of the skill preceded by elements from the competition routine.

All gymnasts are susceptible to *over-use injuries*, such as tenosynovitis, tendinitis, Osgood Schlatters disease. These fairly common injuries are caused by an excessive repetitive load, poor posture, poor technique (particularly upon landings) and sometimes inadequate apparatus. Care should therefore be taken to vary the type of skill, type of support or hang, to avoid lengthy periods on a particular piece of apparatus and to select a varied programme to reduce the likelihood of over-use injuries developing.

4.6   The gymnast's personal clothing and equipment

The general health and safety of the gymnast is the responsibility of both the coach and performer himself. In this respect it is important to ensure that constant checks are made on the performer's dress and equipment with regard to the following:

A.   Clothing

During warm-up it is necessary to wear clothing which will retain the body heat, but it is essential at all times to wear comfortable, close-fitting clothing to reduce the risk of clothing becoming entangled with the apparatus, or handler, and to avoid the dangers of the performer being distracted or momentarily blinded by loose clothing. It is often difficult for a coach to handle or support a gymnast who is wearing loose or Lurex-type, slippery, clothing and these again should be discouraged during training.

Items with buckles and clasps may also lead to injury through scratching or impact upon falling on the clasp or buckle and should not be worn.

B.   Jewellery and grooming

Jewellery such as necklaces, rings, etc., should never be worn during gymnastic activities, since they may distract the vision of the gymnast and also cause scratches. Rings may impair the grip on a piece of apparatus and may damage the apparatus itself.

It is a trait in the sport of gymnastics for all concerned to be well groomed and conscious of their appearance at all times. Long hair should be avoided but at minimum should be safely tied back to avoid distraction and loss of vision. Long hair may also inhibit safe supporting and thus will put the gymnast at risk.

Long fingernails may cause personally inflicted scratches or in the case of the coach may scratch the gymnast during a supporting skill. Well-groomed fingernails are therefore to be considered as part of the safety precautions.

C.   Footwear

Many gymnasts prefer to work barefoot, others in socks alone and others with lightweight gymnastic shoes or slippers. Whatever the choice, they should always be aware of the following factors: the wearing of socks only should never be permitted on polished floors or slippery matted surfaces for running or tumbling since loss of footing is likely and is highly dangerous; when gymnastic shoes are to be worn, ensure that they are in good condition, are well-fitting, and that the soles have non-slip properties.

D.   Handguards

'Handguards' or 'grips' are worn to separate hand skin from the apparatus and thereby reduce the abrasion to the hands, thus reducing the tendency to blister the skin.

The grips are made from a variety of materials such as suede, strong, synthetic materials and leather. Leather is by far the most popular since it retains the hand chalk, is flexible, strong and comfortable to wear once 'broken-in'. The leather must be good quality, free from flaws and strong enough to withstand the heavy demands to which it will be subjected.

The *rough side* of the leather should be placed *away from* the palm of the hand to aid the retention of the chalk and enhance the hand grip on the apparatus. The modern tendency is to develop a 'ruck' in the guard for improved grip on parallel bars and horizontal bar. This is developed by means of a slightly longer grip being worn around the fingertips and the ruck being created in the area of the fingers above the palm of the hand. A small dowel is sometimes worn by advanced gymnasts on horizontal bars for such skills as one-arm giants. Its function is to ensure a more positive grip and transfer a greater load from the hand to the grip to lessen the burning of the skin and thereby prolong the ability to train. *It is essential to check that the length of guard or grip* is not such that the 'loop' or 'ruck' may come into contact with the base of the guard at the other side of the bar. In this situation the two parts of the guard 'bind' together and may 'wrap' or lock on the bar, causing a situation which may lead to serious wrist or hand injury.

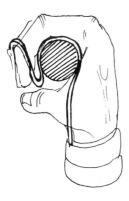

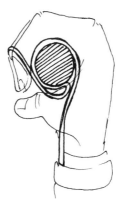

Rucked handguard – correct   Rucked but too long – wrapping incorrect

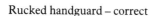

Advanced gymnasts also use a special design of handguard for use on rings. The guard includes a suitable dowel which creates a fold around the ring to assist in holding the hand to the ring. The dowel sits between the fingers and the ring and is held in position by the fold on the ring. Often difficulty is encountered in releasing the grip upon dismounting and for this reason it is advised that beginner gymnasts do not utilise this type of grip on basic skills.

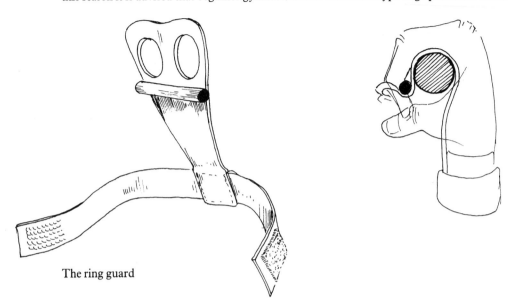

The ring guard

The gymnast must be encouraged to check, daily, the condition of his handguards. Inspection should include the thickness of the guard, are there any cuts or nicks, is the stitching in good condition, is there any damage to buckles and is the surface becoming polished or slippy. A good coach will insist on these daily checks and he will himself carry out frequent spot checks.

E.   Hand chalk

Magnesium carbonate or 'chalk' is applied to the hands to absorb perspiration and hence help the retention of the contact with the apparatus. Magnesium carbonate also helps to reduce friction between the apparatus and the hands (or guards) and helps to prevent blisters.

Insufficient use of chalk will cause loss of grip and will leave dangerous sweaty patches on the apparatus. An excessive use of chalk may cause it to enter the eyes of the performer or coach and should therefore be discouraged. A number of advanced gymnasts prefer to supplement the hand chalk with a light application of resin when performing under bar swings such as giants on parallel bars.

F.   The wearing of spectacles

When a gymnast has the need to wear spectacles he must ensure that they are firmly tied to the head. Many gymnasts successfully wear contact lenses, but it is advisable to choose a durable type which will withstand impact or shock.

G. Hand taping

It is common practice for a gymnast with sore or torn hands to gain further protection by the use of zinc oxide tape strapping. This is quite safe providing the tape is of good quality, is correctly applied and does not impair the hand hold on the apparatus.

The hand should always be taped with strips of tape running up lengthways across the palm of the hand, around the back of the fingers and back down and across the palm of the hand. The tape effectively resembles a hand guard and can be secured by taping over the tape around the wrists. This type of strapping is less likely to roll and will therefore be more reliable than taping around the palm of the hand. Where a blister has occurred, the blistered skin can be removed with sterilised utensils and the area covered with an annular ring of suitable felt. The felt is then held in position by a tape strapping as described above. This type of taping will remove the load from the blistered area and the gymnast may continue work if the discomfort is not too great.

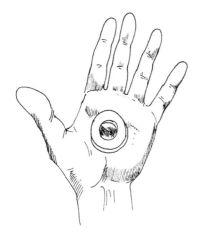 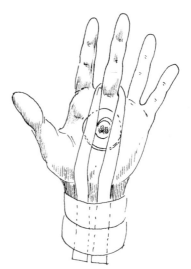

4.7   Assembly and disassembly of apparatus

It is essential that the erection, dismantling and storage of gymnastic equipment is carried out in an orderly and disciplined manner. All methods employed should comply to the manufacturer's instructions. The coach should give clear instructions and must supervise all stages of apparatus movements.

Prior to commencing a session the coach should *check all apparatus* for correct assembly and ensure that all landing surfaces or apparatus 'paddings' are adequate and correctly placed.

Checks should be made on all karabiner fittings, chains, wires, tensioners (for full screw thread location and correct tension), crossed wires, crossed chain links, incorrectly located bars, over-polished bars, damaged mats, and alignment of uprights and apparatus with the building structure. The coach should also ensure that dismantling and storage of the apparatus is carefully carried out to avoid unnecessary accidents.

4.8   General discipline and safety

Accidents in the gymnasium may be caused through ignorance, stupidity and horseplay. It is necessary, therefore, that the discipline and order throughout a gym session should be of a high standard. Gym club rules regarding behaviour should be established and enforced at all times.

Horseplay, practical jokes, unsupervised running around the gym should never be permitted and an orderly movement between apparatus changes should be encouraged.

A good standard of behaviour and presentation will enhance the self-control and discipline traits that all gymnasts require.

5.0 First aid and emergency provision

Whenever gymnastic activities are taking place it is imperative that the following emergency procedures and provisions are accessible and fully understood by all participants.

5.1   The provision

i.   The facility must include a *telephone* together with clear instructions on how to dial out for emergency services.

ii.   A *list of relevant numbers* which should include the nearest *casualty department* should be readily available.

iii. A *First Aid kit* should be to hand and should contain the following:

Pain relieving agents: pain-relieving spray
Cleansing agents: antiseptic cleanser, antiseptic cream, gauze swabs, non-adherent dressing, cotton bandages, cotton wool swabs.
Strapping and bandages: crepe bandages (3-inch and 6-inch), triangular bandage, sponge dressing tape, adhesive bandages (3-inch), roll of cotton wool, zinc oxide tape (½ inch and 1 inch).
Miscellaneous supplies: safety pins, sterile needles (for blisters), eye bath and fluid, inflatable or Kramer splints, clinical thermometer and a *First Aid Manual*.

5.2   The procedure

No matter how careful a coach may be and no matter what precautions are taken accidents will happen. A coach must therefore be prepared to deal with an accident situation. Always bear in mind that you may not be qualified to diagnose or treat injury and that incorrectly applied assistance may have serious consequences.

Perhaps the best advice is to carry out only emergency First Aid and then seek the help of qualified medical personnel. However, the following procedure should be adopted in the event of an accident occurring.

i. Stop the class and direct other members of the class not immediately involved in the accident away from the injured person.

ii. Ensure that the patient is conscious simply by talking to them – if not, check that their breathing rate is stable – if not carry out emergency artificial respiration and seek *immediate Emergency Medical Help*.

iii. If the patient is conscious ascertain from him how the accident happened? How did he fall? Where is the pain located? Test to ensure that there are 'feelings to touch' at legs and arms in the event of a suspected spinal injury.

iv. Look for any signs of obvious deformity of the limbs or joints and abnormality in motion.

v. Seek qualified advice if in doubt at all, or if there are any obvious signs of serious injury.

vi. Only after serious injury has been ruled out should a patient be moved.

The above is only a general guide and it is *strongly recommended that all coaches become fully conversant with the First Aid Manual and, where possible, seek formal training in this area.*

6.0 Caring for the injured gymnast

The following are recommendations for the immediate treatment of injuries, but it is essential always to apply the philosophy that *if in doubt seek qualified assistance.*

6.1 Soft tissue injuries

The majority of sports injuries are soft tissue injuries and include injuries to the skin, muscles, tendons and ligaments.

A. Injuries to the skin

i. *Blisters:* These are frequently caused by new or badly fitting gym shoes and friction on the hand. Clean the area with a mild soap and water and then puncture the blister with a sterile needle. If the blister has 'torn' the skin, remove the ragged edges with sterilised equipment and tape the wound to prevent infection. If it is desired to continue training or competing on a blistered hand, then protective taping can be used as illustrated in section 4.6(g).

ii. *Abrasions:* Clean thoroughly to remove dirt and apply an antiseptic. The wound may be covered by a sterile dressing that will not stick to the wound or smaller abrasions may be left uncovered to permit the formation of a healthy scab.

iii.   *Cuts:* Stop the bleeding by applying pressure directly over the cut, or by squeezing the edges of the cut together. Cleanse the injured area with soap and water or an antiseptic, but *do not* use an antiseptic cream as this impedes the healing of the cut. The cut should be covered with a clean dressing and serious cuts should be referred to a physician.

B.   Injuries to muscles

i.   *Pulled muscle:* Usually involves the tearing of a few muscle fibres due to overload, tiredness or poor warm-up. An ice pack should be applied immediately to reduce bleeding (and increase recovery later) and the muscle rested. The muscle should be protected from further aggravation until it has healed. Remember, pain is an indication that an injury is present and it is foolhardy to ignore the pain and continue further to aggravate the injury. The application of alternative 'hot' and 'cold' treatments after 36 hours will aid the recovery of the injured muscle. This treatment involves alternate periods of soaking or heating the injured muscle in hot water for up to 30 minutes, followed by icing for a few minutes. This causes the blood vessels to dilate and the circulation is improved to disperse the congealed blood from the injured area, thus preventing or reducing 'stiffness' in that area. The muscle can then be gradually stetched to improve the range followed by gradual strengthening.

ii.   *Torn muscle:* A heavy blow or excessive load can cause a large number of muscles fibres to tear resulting in heavy bleeding and painful swelling which restricts movement. The muscle should be immediately iced and elevated and then referred to a physician for treatment followed by physiotherapy.

iii.   *Tendon injuries:* Tendons attach the muscle to the bone. Tendon injuries include tendinitis, an inflamed tendon which is caused by over-use. This commonly affects a gymnast in the wrist, forearm, and Achilles tendon. Icing and rest from that type of activity is recommended until the pain has subsided.

iv.   *Rupture of the tendon:* Violent stress can cause the complete or partial rupture of the tendon. The injury should be iced and referred to a physician.

v.   *Injuries to ligaments:* Ligaments are inelastic fibrous tissues which help stabilise a joint. Those which are most frequently injured are those associated with the knee and ankle joints. Twisting or turning a joint through an abnormal range will result in 'strained' or, more seriously, ruptured ligaments. The injury should be iced, strapped with a compression strapping and elevated to reduce bleeding and then rested for 24 hours. After rest for between 24—72 hours depending on the severity of the injury, the joint movements may be commenced. The range should be gradually increased, within the limitations of pain, over a 7 to 10-day period. *A suspected complete ligament rupture should be immediately referred to a physician.*

vi.   *Bruises:* Bleeding will occur with all soft tissue injuries and a bruise or haematoma will develop. The rate of recovery from an injury will be related to the amount of bleeding, the area of soft tissue affected, and the rate of dispersal of the haematoma or bruise. The application of ice, elevation and rest will reduce the bleeding while the utilisation of 'hot' and 'cold' applications and/or ultrasonic treatment will disperse the bruising more rapidly.

6.2   Injuries to bones and joints

This type of injury may involve bruising of the bone, fracture of the bone or a dislocation of the joint.

    i.   *Bone bruise:* Apply ice pack and, if severe, refer to a physician.

    ii.   *Fracture of bone: Never move an injured person if a fracture of the spine, neck or skull is suspected.* Check for feeling in arms and legs and seek immediate medical help. In the event of a fractured bone in a finger, arm or leg, the intense pain can be relieved by the careful application of a splint or sling. Care should be taken not to disturb the fractured bone. A finger may be strapped to an adjacent finger, a leg splinted to the other leg or the arm strapped to the trunk in a sling to support the weight of the arm. The injured person should be taken directly to an accident department at the nearest hospital.

    iii.   *Dislocation of a joint:* This may occur to any joint in the event of a blow or fall or excessive overload. The joint will be deformed and swelling due to bleeding from ruptured muscles may occur. Apply a support to the injured area to reduce pain and ice pack the injury. *On no account should you attempt to replace the dislocated joint*, as this could cause extensive, serious damage. Refer the injured person to the casualty department at the nearest hospital.

6.3   Injuries due to impact blows

The potential seriousness of *injuries to the brain or spinal cord should never be underestimated.* First Aid can be of extreme importance, but qualified medical help must be sought immediately.

A.   Concussion

A blow to the head may lead to concussion and possible brain damage and great care must be taken in assessing the extent of injuries; if at all in doubt seek medical advice.

The severity of the injury may be assessed as follows:

    i.   Question the patient for loss of memory in personal details, and awareness of events surrounding the injury.

    ii.   Check the vision (near and far) dilated pupils, squinting and eye co-ordination by passing a finger in front of the eyes.

    iii.   Does the patient feel sick or have a headache? Check muscle co-ordination by finger to nose test, standing on one leg or hopping gently.

If concussion is suspected even in the mildest form the following rules should be observed:

Do not permit further participation until medical advice has been sought.

Do not leave the patient alone or permit the consumption of alcohol.

Do not allow the patient to ride a bicycle or drive a car.

Do obtain medical advice.

B.   Coma

The onset of unconsciousness is a situation in which immediate emergency action is essential. If a patient cannot breathe properly serious brain damage can occur.

It is essential that the following procedure is carried out:

   i.   *Check the airway*, remove vomit, and ensure that the tongue has not been 'swallowed'.

   ii. *Place the patient in the 'coma position'*, (i.e. face down, head turned to the side and airway open), ensuring that the head, neck and spine are in a straight line, and that the airway is open.

   iii. *Check the pulse* at the neck or wrist.

   iv. *If breathing is abnormal*, apply mouth to mouth resuscitation.

   v.   *SEND FOR MEDICAL HELP.*

   vi. *Keep the patient warm* and do not leave the patient unattended.

6.4   Spinal cord injuries

Any form of injury to the spinal cord is extremely dangerous and may result in some form of paralysis, or death. Great care should be taken when this form of injury is suspected. The vertebrae of the spine protect the spinal cord and if these are damaged then the spine is unstable and the spinal cord may be vulnerable to injury. Where this type of injury is suspected, *on no account must the injured person be moved without qualified medical supervision.* Mis-handling in this condition could cause further extreme complications to the injury. The symptoms generally associated with spinal injuries are: neck or back pain (although this may not always be felt), loss of power and loss of sensation in the limbs and tingling feelings in the limbs. The following procedure should be adopted if a spinal injury is suspected and *the patient is conscious.*

   i.   Minimise all neck, head and spine movements.

   ii. Ensure that the airway is open and clear.

   iii. Send for medical, emergency assistance.

If it is necessary to roll the patient onto his back, then the spine, neck and head should first be splinted before rolling the complete body simultaneously in a log-rolling technique. If the injured *patient is unconscious* the following should be adopted.

   i.   Minimise all head, neck and spine movements.

   ii. Check the airway is open and clear.

   iii. Send for medical, emergency assistance.

   iv. Splint the spine, head and neck.

   v.   Moving the whole of the body simultaneously, 'log roll' the patient into the coma position.

DO NOT, under any circumstances, permit unqualified persons to administer any form of medical assistance as they may cause further serious damage by moving the patient.

6.5   Other injuries

i.   *Nose bleed:* Keep the patient in an upright, sitting or standing position and cover the nose with cold cloths. If the bleeding is heavy, pinch the nose and place a *small* cotton pack in the nostrils.

ii.   *Damage to teeth:* Save completely removed teeth, and if loosened, cover area with sterile gauze and refer to the dentist.

iii. *Foreign body in the eye:* use an eyebath with copious applications of eye washing fluid to remove offending particle.

iv.   *More serious eye injury:* Cover the eye with a clean dressing and refer the patient to a hospital.

v.   *Injury to testicle:* Lay the injured person on his back and apply ice pack. If the pain does not subside refer to a physician.

REMEMBER, YOU ARE A COACH AND PROBABLY NOT MEDICALLY QUALIFIED SO DO NOT TAKE CHANCES – IF IN DOUBT SEEK QUALIFIED MEDICAL ASSISTANCE.

7.0   Class management

A successful gymnastics class will be one which offers:

i.   A safe environment in which to train.

ii.   The necessary stimulants to motivate the gymnasts.

To achieve this situation it is essential that a meticulously planned *training programme* is implemented and that *good teaching practices* are adopted.

7.1   The structure for a gymnastics session

The lesson plan adopted will be affected by the level of performer, the time available, the number of sessions offered per week, and other salient factors which will be discussed later in this chapter. However, the following outline is a general format which will serve as the basis for the majority of club, school, or recreational classes.

a.   *Erect and check all apparatus* to be used in the session. Ensure that the height and width settings of the apparatus are suitable for the age and level of ability of the students in the class.

b.   *Introduction and aims of the session:* Set out clearly the format and aims of the session so all concerned are aware of their tasks.

c.   *Conduct the warm-up:* The warm-up period should precede all gymnastics activities and should always be supervised, to ensure that it is adequately conducted. The warm-up should amount to approximately 10% of the duration of the class time, or at least 10 minutes when the duration of the session is limited.

See Sections 11.0 – 11.3 for greater detail concerning the structure and benefits of the warm-up.

d.   *Preparation and orientation period:* In this period skills are rehearsed which relate closely to those elements which are to be taught in the main section of the lesson. These skills may include stretching for mobility, landing techniques, simulation skills, spatial awareness skills and timer skills. The inclusion of this aspect of preparation into the session will reduce anxiety in the gymnast and will ensure both a mental and physical preparedness for the elements to be learnt later in the session. The duration of this period will be between 15–20% of the session.

e.   *The main topic area:* This period is devoted to the learning of gymnastics skills, elements, combinations and exercises and will be the main object of the session.

f.   *Conditioning:* As with mobility training, it is better if this aspect of training can be undertaken in a separate session. If this is not possible it should follow the Main Topic Area of the session and should be designed to suit the needs of the individual performers with respect to age characteristics and strength weaknesses. Conditioning elements and programmes are dealt with in more detail in Sections 12.5 and 12.6.

g.   *The warm-down:* In order to reduce the level of lactic acid build-up in the muscles and to return the cardiovascular and respiratory systems to normal, a period of light exercise and stretching is recommended following the heavier aspects of training.

h.   *Dismantling the apparatus:* Instruction on the safe handling of the apparatus must be given and the dismantling, handling and storage of equipment must be supervised at all times. It is good practice to ensure that 'when you leave the gym it is in the state in which a good coach would wish to find it'.

i.   *Appraisal of the session:* It is good practice at the end of the session to reflect upon the degree of success of the performers, emphasising good points and offering encouragement to overcome areas of weakness. This will motivate the gymnasts towards achieving their goals in future sessions.

7.2   Teaching guidelines for the coach

A coach will develop his own teaching technique around his own personality, but the following factors will serve as a guideline to good teaching practice.

A.   Supervision

Supervision is one of the most critical elements in establishing a safe training environment. Supervision may be 'general' or 'specific' in nature.

i.   *General supervision:* This involves giving direction to a whole range of activities taking place within a lesson. It is applied when a fair number of students are being taught and it will be necessary to select carefully the content of the skills to be taught since individual spotting and guidance will not be possible.

ii.   *Specific supervision:* when a smaller group of students is being taught the teaching can be directed towards the individual, within the group. Since individual handling is possible, more advanced skill progressions can be taught.

iii.   *General guidelines:*

   a.   Be present, and immediately accessible at all times when a session is in progress.
   b.   Be alert to potential problems.
   c.   Ensure that all assisting coaches are conversant with and competent to do all the work allocated to them.
   d.   Observe from an unobstructed position.
   e.   Maintain a controlled type of discipline.
   f.   Be aware of the onset of fatigue and boredom in order to avoid possible accidents.

B.   Class control

Class control, without regimentation, will minimise accidents and will complement the motivational aspects of a class.

   i.   Ensure that you can clearly observe the whole class at all times.

   ii.   To obtain the attention of the class shout clearly 'stop' or 'hold it' or similar expressions. Ensure all activity stops and that attention is drawn towards you.

   iii.   Having ascertained that the instructions are clearly understood commence the activity again by use of such phrases as 'OK start' or 'Begin again', 'Carry on working'.

   iv.   Behavioural regulations should be introduced and they should be applied equally to all participants.

C.   Communication

   i.   Arrange the class in such a way that they can clearly see and hear your introduction or instructions. Ensure also that there is adequate space for manoeuvring between groups.

   ii.   When introducing a new skill use a visual demonstration: 'Actions speak louder than words'. A live demonstration by a performer will provide motivation and instil confidence in other members of the class.

   iii.   Always give clear and precise uncomplicated instructions and make allowances for the different ages and varying educational levels of the performers.

   iv.   Ensure that the gymnasts and staff fully understand the instructions given to them.

   v.   Use visual aids, such as a live demonstration, photograph, video tape or film to enable the gymnast to visualise the skill you wish him to perform.

   vi.   Offer praise and carefully applied objective criticism in order to motivate the gymnasts and assist coaches.

   vii.   Utilise techniques in developing rhythm and timing with the learning of skills.

   viii.   Recapitulate on visualisation and mental rehearsal of the technique or skill to reinforce the instructions being given.

D.   Progressive skills

    i.   To ensure the safe and successful learning of gymnastic elements, it is essential that carefully selected, progressive skills are taught. Seek the advice of a more experienced coach.

    ii.   The gymnast must successfully execute each skill before being allowed to progress to the next skill. Remember, a short cut in the learning stages will mean a deficiency in the complete understanding of an advanced skill at a later date.

    iii.   The coach should control the level of skill according to a realistic appraisal of the gymnast's skill, strength and courage.

    iv.   Ensure that the activity or skill is appropriate to the age, sex, size and ability of the gymnast.

    v.   Continually vary the training schedule in order to present the skills in a slightly different, but still related, manner. This will maintain the enthusiasm of the participant.

    vi.   Limitations on strength or physical preparedness should be identified and the gymnast motivated towards specific physical improvements.

Further guidance on the selection of progressive teaching skills will be found in the later sections on the teaching of specific gymnastic elements.

7.3   Factors influencing learning

If a coach is to be effective then he must have an understanding of those factors that influence the learning process and aid the motivation of the gymnast. This will necessitate familiarity with the following psychological facets.

A.   Goal setting

One of the most extensively used tools in motivating performers is the setting of 'aims' or 'goals' which the gymnast must strive to achieve. If the goals are correctly set and the gymnast achieves them with the appropriate level of effort then he will gain in confidence and will be inspired towards higher goals.

The level of goal setting is critical and the following guidelines should be followed.

    i.   The goals must be 'short-term' and must relate to the required long-term aim in performance.

    ii.   The goals must be specific and precise.

    iii.   The goal must place sufficient demands upon the performer that when the goal is achieved he has experienced satisfaction and is motivated towards a higher goal. If the demands set by the 'goal' are insufficient they will cease to motivate the performer.

    iv.   The goals must be related to performance so that their achievement can be used as a guideline to performance.

    v.   Goal setting will only be successful if both the coach and the performer understand the goals clearly and feedback is offered to motivate the performer.

    vi.   The goals must be accepted by the performer and should only be set by joint discussion between the performer and the coach.

    vii.   The goal must be within the control of the performer, i.e. a target score on a particular apparatus or overall score is in control of the gymnast but a final overall placing is largely in the hands of his fellow competitors.

    viii.   The performer must believe he has a 50% chance of achieving the goal. If he has only a 20% chance the goal is too high and he will fail – particularly under the stress of competition.

    ix.   The goal must be realistic enough to avoid frustration due to repeated failure.

    For instance, if the following goals were set and the gymnast's performance improved as shown he would still experience frustration because the goal set was too high.

Goal	Achievement
5 successes out of 5	5 achieved
6 successes out of 6	6 achieved
8 successes out of 10	7 achieved

    It would be of greater motivational effect if the goals were reduced to become attainable as follows:

3 successes out of 5	4 achieved
5 successes out of 8	6 achieved
7 successes out of 10	7 achieved

    x.   It is also of value if the degree of acceptability of quality of performance is also clearly stated for assessing the achievement level of the goals.

B.   Differences in personality and emotion

The coach needs to be aware of the differences in personality of his performer and must be sympathetic towards the individual psychological make-up of the performer.

The personality factors to consider are:

    i.   *Extroverts:* generally outgoing types demonstrating confidence.

    ii.   *Introverts:* usually quiet and withdrawn.

    iii.   *Introverted extrovert:* usually very quiet and unassuming but can in the right environment become very much an extrovert.

    iv.   *Neurotic:* very nervous type.

    v.   *Hypochondriac:* suffering from depression or over-sensitive to pain or injury.

The coach must be familiar with the personality traits of each gymnast and must learn to consider carefully the type of feedback he offers to the individual.

What might be trivial to one person might be of immense importance to another and a particular comment to one performer might be inspirational, but may mean disaster to another.

A coach must also become sympathetic to the various emotional responses expressed by the performers and should attempt to help the performer cope with a variety of situations. Emotional outbursts may arise through the advent of puberty, together with other external conflicts with parents, work, love, financial problems, school work, etc. An understanding coach will be available for consultation on these matters and will make due allowance for these emotional situations.

C.   Motivation

Motivation is the medium through which a gymnast gains incentive or inspiration to reach a goal. This motivation may be classified in two categories:

i.   *'Intrinsic' motivation:* The self-motivation for learning which is derived from the satisfying fulfilment felt by the gymnast. This intrinsic motivation may be related to the self-determination to succeed and it is this form of self-motivation which the coach should strive to develop.

ii.   *'Extrinsic' motivation:* These motivations are imposed upon the performer by the coach, the parents and fellow gymnasts. If the gymnast performs because he feels he ought to because it is the desire of the coach or parents, then he will not gain true fulfilment.

The external influences may be counter-productive and it is self-motivation that makes a successful performer. The coach must motivate the gymnast by making the training and competition enjoyable and satisfying rather than offering external rewards.

The setting of well-chosen goals will help to motivate the gymnast, particularly if the gymnast is consulted in the setting of the goals.

D.   Providing feedback

The coach often takes the role of the camera and offers feedback on performance to the gymnast in the form of verbal comments or preferably in pictorial form such as a drawing. It is important that the feedback can be clearly interpreted and that it is offered only after a delay of around eight seconds after the performance. This will allow the coach to think carefully about the performance and his intended feedback and the gymnast will be ready to receive the comments.

Ensure that the comments are always 'positive' in that they will provide encouragement and refrain from using 'negative' feedback comments which can be distructive.

Always try to be complimentary and offer frequent positive, reinforcing comments during the early learning stages.

With more mature gymnasts it is recommended that the frequency of feedback comments is gradually reduced and the gymnast encouraged to employ 'self-appraisal' of his own performance. Remember that no feedback may be interpreted as negative reinforcement, hence it is necessary gradually to reduce the frequency, and to make positive comments from time to time.

The following pattern of feedback is recommended to develop the gymnast towards a state of self-sufficiency.

a.   Early stage of learning: frequent positive feedback.
b.   Middle stages of learning: comment only after a series of attempts.
c.   Later stages of learning: irregular and infrequent positive comments.

8.0 Planning the training

Unplanned training sessions, routines constructed without forethought, and carelessly selected skills will seriously prejudice the successful development of a gymnast.

To enable a gymnast to realise his full potential he must operate within a meticulously planned *training programme*. Only through an organised programme and carefully selected *training schedules* will the gymnast make the desired progress.

Frequent evaluation of competition results and training sessions will evidence weaknesses and enable the training schedules to be modified to eliminate those weaknesses.

8.1 Long-term planning

A. The long-term programme

It is essential to 'look to the future' when setting out a training programme. This is done by predicting the likely competition programme for a period of up to four years in order to set out the programme or calendar. Once this *'long-term programme'* is established the intermediary year's programmes can be set out and from this, monthly, weekly, and even daily sessions can be structured.

B. The long-term schedule

Having selected the major competitions within the long-term programme, it is possible to predict the routines and elements which it is hoped the gymnast will perform at those events. By making such predictions it is now possible to select intermediary stages of learning and skill developments which will culminate in the performance of the desired routines.

8.2 Short-term planning

A. The short-term programme

With the long-term programme (calendar) set out, it is now possible to set out the programme to show the type of training schedule to be introduced during a particular period of training. This aspect of planning is usually called 'Periodisation of Training' and in the sport of gymnastics two complete cycles of the programme are used per year to meet the two-season calendar.

ONE-YEAR TRAINING PROGRAMME

Element training	*Pre-competition training*	*Competition period*	*Rest*	*Element training*	*Pre-comp. training*	*Comp. period*	*Rest*
1	2	3	4	as 1	as 2	as 3	as 4
Individual elements and combinations + General conditioning	Combinations + Part routines + General and specific conditioning	Full routines + Specific conditioning	ACTIVE REST				

It can be seen from the diagram that the periods are set out to include periods of training through:

    i.   *Element training:* and concentrated general conditioning.

    ii.   *Pre-competition training:* of combinations and part routines together with general and specific conditioning.

    iii.   *Competition period:* where complete routines and areas of instability are practised together with specific conditioning.

    iv.   *Active rest period:* where a change in physical activity is introduced to allow the gymnast to recover from the competition stresses.

It is good advice to 'tail off' the heavy training of routines some 7–10 days prior to a competition in order that 'quality' in performance can be emphasised and to allow the gymnast to prepare mentally for the competition. It is, however, essential to study the preparation of your gymnasts in order to determine the type of 'build-up' that is best suited to that individual gymnast, in order for him to 'peak' at a particular event.

B.   The short-term schedule

With the long-term prediction of routines and elements prepared, this can now be used to set out the progressive training schedules which will eventually produce the desired results.

To prepare these schedules the coach must compile the following information:

    i.   The number of sessions and hours for training available per week.

    ii.   How many sessions to be worked on each apparatus or aspect per week, i.e. dance, conditioning, trampoline, floor, etc.

    iii.   A carefully selected list of the skill, elements and combinations.

The age and ability of the gymnast must be carefully considered when selecting the type of skill and the duration of each training period. A period of between 20–30 minutes per apparatus is recommended for younger gymnasts as this would avoid over-use injuries developing through over-long training periods. The training schedules can now be compiled to show the date, session, apparatus, skills/elements, number of repetitions per session and some easy form of success appraisal.

Once established, the schedules should be strictly adhered to, but frequently analysed to pinpoint weaknesses in the schedule. The use of planned training programmes and schedules will not only ensure the correct development of the gymnast, but will also serve to motivate the gymnasts and coaches. They can easily see the effectiveness of their training and have a clear indication of the future direction of their development by reference to the long-term planning.

9.0 Mechanical principles

'Biomechanics is the scientific study of the application of Mechanical Principles to the movement of the human body.' An understanding of these principles will enhance the appreciation of gymnastics techniques and will greatly reduce the time spent on 'trial and error' or misdirected coaching.

9.1 Definitions of basic terminology

Mass: 'The amount of matter a body possesses'
Mass is measured in kilogrammes (kg).

Weight: 'The property a body has due to it being attracted towards the earth by the effect of gravitational force'

The weight of a body will depend upon its mass, but if the body were in a vacuum or free space it would not be influenced by the force of gravity. The body might have no weight, but it would still have mass.

Mass and weight are two separate entities which can be individually defined, but in 'basic' biomechanics the effect of gravity will always be present and we may consider mass and weight as being similar.

Gravity: 'The attractive force the earth exerts upon a body'
The 'gravitational force' will accelerate a falling body at the rate of 9.81 m/sec/sec. It will also decelerate (retard) a rising body at a similar rate.

Force: 'Is that medium (push or pull) which will move or attempt to move a body'
Units of force are Newtons – 'internal force' is produced by muscular action whilst 'external force' is produced by gravity, friction, ground upthrusts or apparatus reaction.

Velocity: 'Is a measure of how fast a body is moving in a given direction'
i.e. The rate at which distance is travelled in a given direction – metres per second.

Acceleration: 'The rate of change of velocity'
The rate at which a body is speeding up.

Deceleration (or Retardation)
Is the rate at which a body is slowing down.

Energy: 'Is the capacity to do work'
Energy can be stored in a body as *kinetic energy* (moving energy); *potential energy* (due to the position of a body); or *elastic or strain energy* (due to the elastic deformation of the body).

Work: 'Work is done when a force is applied to move a body (mass) through a given distance'

Work done = force × distance moved. When work is done energy is spent.

Power: 'Is the rate at which work is done'

Power is the work done in a given time.

Momentum: 'The quality a body possesses due to its motion'

Momentum = body mass × its velocity.

The greater the velocity (or mass) the greater the momentum.

Impulse: 'A force applied to a body for a short period of time will impart an impulse upon that body'

Impulse = force × period of time.

Impact: 'When two bodies collide they are said to impact'

Elasticity: 'The property of a body to return to its normal state after it has been distorted'

A springboard is deformed upon impact but will quickly return to its original shape due to its elasticity.

9.2 Newton's Laws of Motion

A body at any given time must be in a state of either rest or motion. This state of rest or motion can only be changed by the application of force. The principles governing the effects of force upon motion were stated by Sir Isaac Newton and are fundamental to the study of motion.

Newton's 'three laws of motion' were based upon solid objects which are not capable of developing internal forces. The human body can develop its own forces and hence the study of motion of the human body is a complete study. However, Newton's laws can be applied to give a good understanding of mechanical principles of motion. The following laws of motion can be effectively applied to studies of 'Linear Motion' (straight line motion) or 'Angular Motion' (rotational motion).

In the study of gymnastics techniques we can consider the movement of the centre of gravity to be experiencing straight line motion.

A. Newton's First Law of Motion – The Law of Inertia

'A body will remain in a state of rest or uniform motion in a straight line unless acted upon by an external force'

In simple terms this may be expressed as: 'A force is necessary to produce movement and a force is necessary to change the velocity of a body.'

Examples in the application of Newton's First Law of Motion:

i. *Changing from a state of rest into motion:* A gymnast in a static headstand (at rest) applies muscular force to straighten the arms in pushing the body to handstand. Thus the force has produced motion.

ii.   *Changing the velocity of a body:* The rotational velocity (angular velocity) of the body of a gymnast during the execution of a handspring can be increased by the vigorous drive of the rear leg through the handstand phase. Without this added muscular force (provided by the gluteals and hamstring muscles) the body would have continued with uniform motion (i.e. constant velocity).

iii. *Changing the direction of motion:* The application of a thrust through the arms during a handspring vault will cause the flight path of the body to be elevated above the horse. A muscular contraction causes the thrust which results in a change of direction.

i.   Force producing   ii.   Force increasing velocity
     motion

iii.   Force changing direction

The mathematical equations covered by Newton's First Law of Motion are:

$$Velocity = \frac{distance\ moved}{time\ taken}$$

$$Acceleration = \frac{change\ in\ velocity}{time\ taken}$$

$$Momentum = mass \times velocity$$

B.   Newton's Second Law of Motion – The Law of Acceleration

'The velocity of a moving body will remain constant unless acted upon by an external force'

The rate of change of velocity (acceleration or retardation) of a body is proportional to the force acting on it and the change will take place in the direction of a resultant force.

   i.   The stronger the musuclar contraction of the triceps muscle during a press-up the quicker the body will rise in the direction of the applied force. The greater the force, the greater the change in velocity.

   ii.   During the contact with a springboard for vault take-off the body has an element of forwards rotation. The depression of the board will, by reason of its elasticity, impart a force to the body which will increase its rotational velocity in a forwards direction.

Increased forward rotation through the application of the elastic force from the board to the body.

If we consider that the mass of a gymnast's body will remain constant and that *momentum is the product of mass × velocity*, then, since it is the magnitude of the applied force which will determine the change in velocity, we can state that:

The rate of change of momentum is proportional to the force causing that change.

The momentum of a gymnast can only change if the velocity changes (i.e. acceleration or deceleration), since the mass is constant; thus:

$$\text{Change in momentum} = \text{mass} \times \text{change in velocity}$$

This then implies that:

$$\text{Force} = \text{mass} \times \text{change in velocity}$$
$$\text{or}$$
$$\textit{Force} = \textit{mass} \times \textit{acceleration}$$

Hence: *The greater the applied force, the greater the change in velocity* (acceleration or deceleration).

The implications of Newton's Second Law of Motion

i.   To accelerate a body we must apply a force. The rate of increase in velocity will be proportional to the force.

ii. It will require a greater force to accelerate a heavier body and similarly a greater force to slow the heavier body down. (It is easier to accelerate and stop a car than a heavy lorry.)

iii. The direction of the acceleration will be in the direction of the resultant force.

iv. To decelerate a body we must apply a suitable force in opposition to the direction of motion.

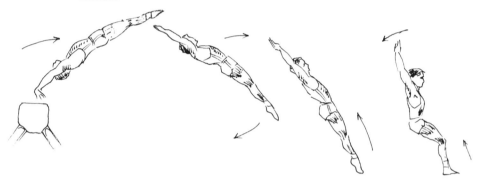

The application of force upon landing to 'kill' rotation

v.   During the strength conditioning programme we increase the strength and power of the muscles to improve the force they can provide and the speed at which they can apply that force. Since the force will be greater we can cause increased acceleration of the body in the execution of gymnastic skills.

vi. A gymnast descending from handstand on the horizontal bar will be accelerated by the force of gravity and momentum will be gained. A heavy body will accelerate at the same rate as a lighter body and the same velocity will be achieved. However, the heavier body, with a greater mass, will gain a greater momentum.

Change in momentum = mass × change in velocity

gravitational force

maximum velocity and
maximum momentum at this point

vii.   It is important to note the 'Principle of Conservation of Momentum' which states that *'momentum can only be created by the application of a force and can only be destroyed by the application of a force'*. Reference to the gain in momentum due to the force of gravity in a longswing in (vi) above and to the deceleration during landing in (iv) will illustrate this principle.

C.   Newton's Third Law of Motion – The Law of Action and Reaction

'For every action there is always an equal and opposite reaction'

i.   When a gymnast thrusts against the floor in the take-off for a back somersault or jump there is an equal and opposite reaction from the floor to create elevation.

ii.   Similarly, in the thrust from the hands in a handspring vault there is an equal and opposite reaction from the horse to cause elevation.

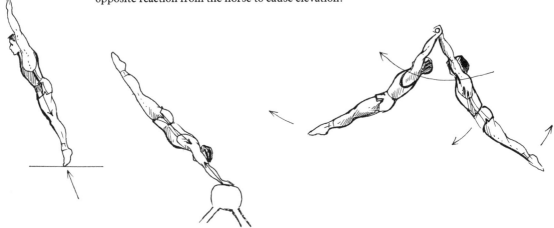

iii.   The action of arching the body while passing under the bar will produce a reaction through the body, to allow the feet to be accelerated into the dish shape for commencement up the upswing.

9.3   Centre of gravity

The centre of gravity is that point at which all the mass of a body can be considered to act.

It is the point at which the body can be supported to keep it on balance.

A.   The position of the centre of gravity for different body shapes

The point of balance (the centre of gravity or C of G) of a body will vary according to the shape of the body and may in fact lie outside the body. The following diagrams illustrate the approximate position of the C of G for common gymnastic shapes.

B.   The centre of gravity and the principles of balance and stability

i.   *To hold a static 'on balance' position the centre of gravity of the body must be directly above (or below) the point of support.*

ii. *If the centre of gravity moves outside the area of the support point it will be off-balance and movement will occur.*

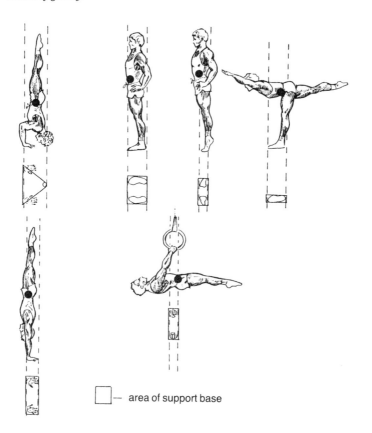

— area of support base

iii. *The greater the area of the support base the easier it is to remain on balance.* The triangular support for a headstand provides a large area of support and the headstand will remain on balance provided the C of G remains inside the triangle.

If we stand on our toes, or on one foot, or one hand, the area of the support base is much smaller and it is therefore more difficult to remain on balance.

iv. *The closer the centre of gravity is to the support base the more 'stable' it will be.*

The higher the centre of gravity is above the support base, the less stable it will be.

The 'straight' body headstand is less stable than the tucked headstand because the centre of gravity is higher above the support.

C.   The centre of gravity and the application of force

According to Newton's First Law of Motion, a body will remain in a state of rest or uniform motion unless acted upon by an external force. If, then, we apply a force to the body as the result of a reaction from the apparatus we can cause the body to move or change in velocity and direction. The direction in which the body moves will be influenced by:

   a.   The magnitude and point of application of the force with respect to the centre of gravity.

   b.   The velocity of the body.

   i.   *The point of application of the force–rotation*

   a.   If the force acts through the centre of gravity it will cause the body to move in a straight line (linear motion). The force is said to act 'concentrically' to the C of G.

Vertical jump

In the diagram the force acts directly below the C of G and is therefore a concentric force. The body will rise and fall in a vertical line.

force

   b.   If the force acts at a point which does not pass through the C of G, the force is said to be an 'eccentric' force and this will cause rotation.

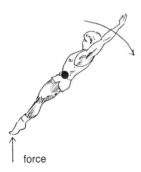

force

Backwards rotation

The force acts in front of the centre of gravity.

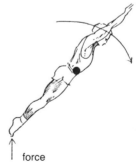

force

Forwards rotatation

The force acts behind the centre of gravity.

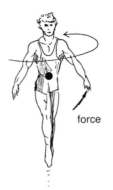

Twisting

The force acting away from the centre of gravity will turn the body.

ii.   The flight path and the effect of force

The flight path of a body can only be influenced during contact with the apparatus, since the external force will come from a reaction from the apparatus.

The magnitude of the force and the direction of its application with respect to the centre of gravity will determine the direction of flight, the height, the time in the air, and the degree of rotation.

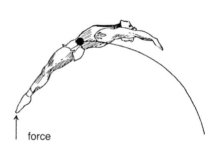

a.   High flight but little rotation.   b.   Low flight but large rotation.

The greater the force, the greater the height and/or rotation. The initial velocity of the moving body will also affect the flight path. The greater the velocity the greater the flight, but the force required to affect a displacement must also be greater.

The following diagram illustrates the flight path of the centre of gravity for various angles of take-off.

A take-off angle of 60° has greatest height and flight time but least rotation.

A take-off angle of 45° has greatest distance.

A take-off angle of 30° has the same distance as a 60° take-off, but less height and flight time.

The time taken to rise is equal to the time taken to fall.

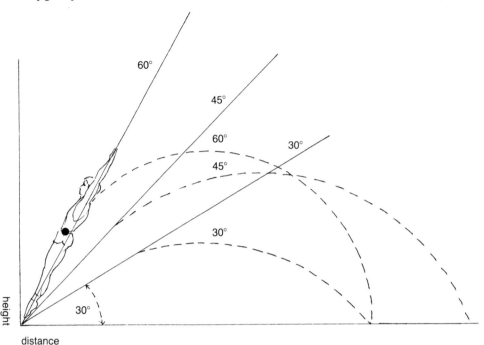

height

distance

To perform rotational elements such as somersaults, we need sufficient time in the air to complete the rotation. The take off at 60° would give the required flight time since a suitable height would be gained and a degree of rotation is also established.

An increase in horizontal velocity at take-off will create greater height, flight time and rotation.

Remember: *The flight path can only be influenced while in contact with the apparatus. Once the body leaves the apparatus the flight path has been established and cannot be altered whilst the body is in flight.*

D.   **Principles of rotation**

i.   *When in contact with an apparatus the body will pivot about the point of contact.*

Rotation in contact with the apparatus

ii.   *When a body is in flight the body will rotate about the centre of gravity.*

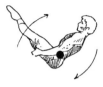

Dive roll – slow rotation   *Tucked front salto* – fast   *Pike back salto* – medium
                                     rotation   rotation

iii.   *The closer the body mass is to the point of rotation the faster it will rotate and vice versa.*

i.e. a tucked body will rotate faster than a straight body. This is the reason why a gymnast who lacks rotation will intuitively bend the legs to create faster rotation.

E.   An understanding of flight path

Since a body will rotate about the centre of gravity when in flight it is necessary for the coach and gymnast to be aware of the path the centre of gravity will follow when in flight. The following principles will apply.

i.   The parabolic flight path

Once in flight the centre of gravity will follow a curved flight path known as the 'parabolic curve'.

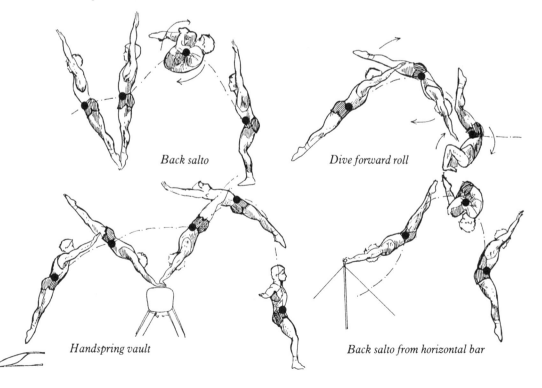

Back salto   *Dive forward roll*

Handspring vault   *Back salto from horizontal bar*

The flight path will be dictated by: the angle of take-off (or release); the direction of the force with respect to the centre of gravity; the velocity of the body at take-off or release; and the height of the body above the landing surface at the point of take-off.

Examples of flight path

i.   *Handspring vault*

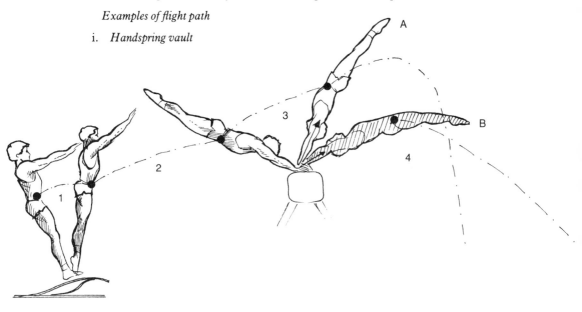

Analysis of the vault:

Phase 1   *Take-off:* During contact with the board the body pivots around the feet. The depression of the board imparts a force to the body upon its return. The direction of the flight on to the horse is determined by the velocity at take-off, the force exerted by the board upon the body and the position of the centre of gravity with respect to the force at take-off.

Phase 2   *Flight on:* The body rotates about the centre of gravity and follows a parabolic curve flight path.

Phase 3   *Thrust:* During contact with the horse the body rotates about the hands and the muscular force exerted by the body upon the horse produces the reaction force from the horse up the body. Again, the position of the centre of gravity with respect to the reaction force and the velocity of the body upon take-off will determine the path for flight off. Position A would give a higher flight while position B would cause lower, longer flight.

Phase 4   *Flight off:* During flight off the body will rotate about the centre of gravity and the flight path will be a parabolic curve (see overleaf).

ii.   *The swinging release from horizontal bar*

During the upward swing on the horizontal bar the body is swinging about a fixed point (the hands) and the centre of gravity will have a given path around the bar. However, upon release of the hand grasp the centre of gravity will enter into a parabolic curve flight path. The direction immediately following release will be at a tangent to (at right angles to) a line drawn through the centre of gravity to the bar at the moment of release. Thus, an early release, A, will produce a low and long flight path while a later release, B, will cause a higher and shorter flight path. Upon release of the grasp the body will rotate about the centre of gravity.

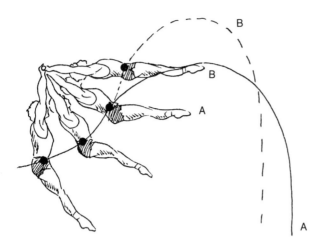

F.   Simple analysis of basic gymnastics movements

i.   The backward giant swing on horizontal bar

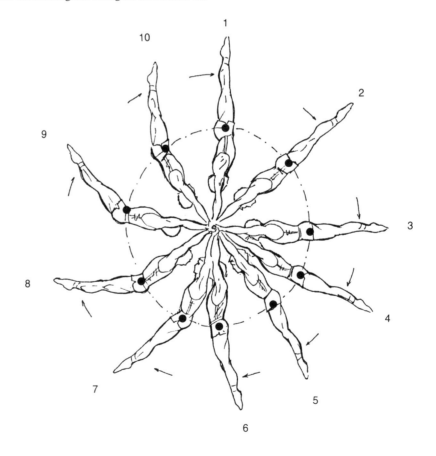

a.   During the downswing from position 1 to 4 the body is pressed away from the bar to move the centre of gravity away from the bar. This enables the force of gravity to have maximum effect in accelerating the body to gain maximum momentum.

b.   At position 5, the hips have been accelerated ahead of the feet to create a hollow body. The tension created in this 'action' is then released to permit the 'reaction' to drive the feet quickly and strongly into a dish shape at position 7.

c.   As the upswing commences, the force of gravity attempts to decelerate the body. To reduce this effect the centre of gravity is brought closer to the bar by closing the shoulder angle and hip angle. These angles are held in to maintain the momentum during the upswing between 7 and 10.

d.   The shoulder angle is now opened in readiness for the downswing but the dished shape is held across the bar to maintain the swing.

The study of the giant swing has now evidenced another important principle, with which the coach and gymnast must be familiar:

When working with gravity the body should be lengthened, but when working against gravity the body must be shortened to maintain momentum.

ii.   The dive forward roll

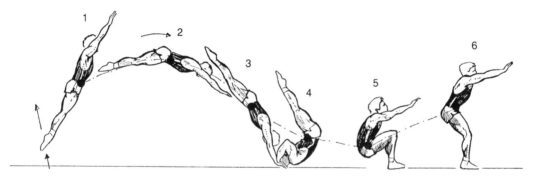

The thrust through the legs and thus the reaction from the floor acts behind the centre of gravity at position 1 and developes both height and rotation in creating the parabolic flight path.

During this flight from 1 to 3 rotation about the centre of gravity is slow since the body creates a long lever. However, upon contact with the hands on the floor, the arms bend, the chin tucks in and the body progressively curls into a tucked position. This reduces the body levers about the centre of gravity and the rotation accelerates, between 4 and 5.

The body is then progressively extended during the standing phase at 5 to reduce rotation. A force is applied through the legs to enable the reaction from the floor to oppose the forward rotation and decelerate the body.

Coaches are encouraged to make further attempts to analyse gymnastics movements to further enhance their understanding of gymnastics techniques.

10.0 Anatomy and physiology

10.1 Age characteristics

It is advisable for all coaches and teachers to be familiar with the natural process of growth and corresponding age characteristics of children. This knowledge will encourage a thorough and safe development programme. The following points should therefore be digested and considered at all stages of development.

a. It is generally accepted that, through lack of sufficient development of the nervous sytem, a child will not normally develop free and co-ordinated movement until the age of seven years has been attained. Similarly the powers of concentration will develop with age and consequently the performance of the gymnastics movements will be somewhat erratic and only achieved through numerous repetitions.

b. It has been established that the ability of a growing child to perform 'motor-functions' is directly related to the age of the child and that it constantly develops to its most intensive period of formation between the ages of twelve to fourteen years.

c. Another age characteristic which must be appreciated when considering young children is the process of bone ossification. This conversion of cartilage into bone is a continual process which is often extended to around the age of nine years. However, a lesser degree of ossification will continue during the growth of bones which is not usually completed until about sixteen to eighteen years in females and eighteen to twenty-one years in males. In fact, the last of the limb bones to stop growing is the clavicle which usually ends at around twenty-five years.

d. This development of the skeletal system together with the growth of the other elements and organs within the body does not generally follow a steady pattern in young children. The growth of the body is somewhat erratic in that it develops in spurts, comprising of increases in height, length, width, increases in body mass, gains and loss in strength and co-ordination. This period of *adolescent growth spurts* plays havoc with the development of the young gymnast. During periods of rapid growth the increased length of bone effects the skeletal levers, and if the gain in strength is not in proportion, the gymnast will experience loss in co-ordination, apparent loss of strength, and an inability to perform skills which he was previously able to achieve. This effect of the growth spurts can have a detrimental psychological effect upon the gymnast and a knowledgeable coach will alleviate the situation by:

   i.   Being aware of the onset of an adolescent growth spurt.

   ii. Explaining to the young gymnast why he is experiencing the various problems.

   iii. Being more tolerant and understanding during this period and amending the training programmes accordingly to alleviate anxiety.

e. A body's capabilities will develop with increased demands upon the body, but it should be remembered that the spine of a young person is extremely flexibile and the supporting muscles are generally quite elastic. Care should be taken not to physically over-stress a young child. Remember also that the body's capabilities will depreciate with insufficient or excessive demands placed upon it.

f. During the period of adolescent growth a trained gymnast will develop a degree of muscular strength which is in advance of the development of the skeletal bone. This may result in small particles of bone being pulled away from the outside of the bone around the area of insertion of the muscle. One such example is Osgood Schlatters disease where the continued strong contractions of the quadriceps muscle may cause the flaking of the bone on the shin just below the knee. The injury is not usually serious, but the caring coach, upon the evidence of pain in that area, will seek medical advice and will amend the training accordingly.

g. The onset of puberty will also place emotional and psychological stresses upon the gymnast. The coach must be patient and understanding during this period when the gymnast may behave erratically and emotionally.

h. There is a great deal of evidence to suggest that young girls are naturally more flexible than boys and it will generally require greater periods of training to achieve good flexibility in a male gymnast. However, the male is usually stronger than the female and the young boy may be expected to develop in this aspect of training to a greater level.

10.2 The basic structure of a joint

A joint will comprise of the following:

a. *Bone:* An assembly of two or more bones to allow movement of the bones.

b. *Articular cartilage:* Covers the end of the bones to provide a smooth articular surface.

c. *Fibro cartilage:* Separates the bones and is a dense form of cartilage which is basically a shock absorber and sliding surface.

d. *Synovial membrane:* This thin layer of tissue lines a joint and produces a fluid (synovial fluid) to lubricate the joint surfaces.

e. *Ligaments:* These are made from a strong fibrous material and are attached across the joint to stabilise and reinforce the joint.

f. *Tendons:* The end of a muscle tapers into tendons which in turn attach the muscle to the bone.

g. *Muscles:* Muscles are stimulated by the nervous system and contract (or relax) to cause articulation of the bones in the joint.

Synovial joints are the lubricated joints, which allow relatively free movement in the joint, while *cartilaginous* joints comprising of the tougher fibro cartilage are seen when lesser movement is required – i.e. the vertebrae of the spine are separated by fibro cartilage discs.

A simple example of a synovial joint appears on the following page.

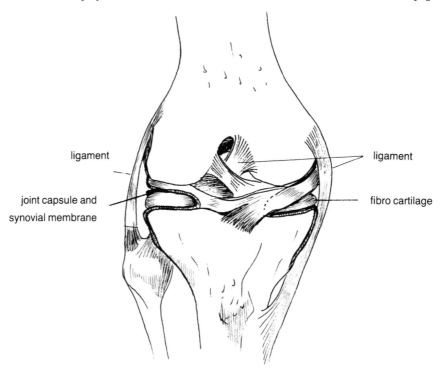

10.3   The function of muscles

Muscles are stimulated by impulses from the nervous system to cause them to contract (or relax) to move the limbs or bones in a joint complex. In simple terms muscles can be said to work in pairs: when one muscle contracts its opposite partner will simultaneously relax to permit the controlled movement of the limb. The limb will move in the direction of the contracting muscle (the agonist or protagonist) while the opposite muscle (the antagonist) relaxes at a controlled rate to maintain a controlled movement of the limb.

The elbow joint shown offers a useful example.

During 'flexion' of the elbow the *biceps muscle contracts* while the *triceps muscle relaxes*. During 'extension' of the elbow they play the opposite role in that the triceps contracts and the biceps relaxes.

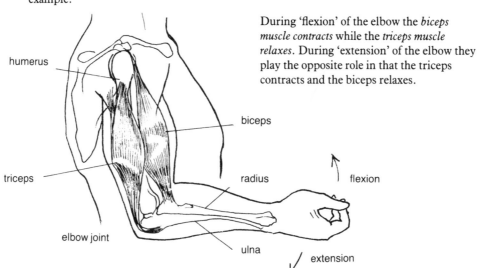

10.4   Types of muscle contraction

When one muscle is stimulated by the nervous system its opposite partner will behave in an equally opposite manner to maintain a control in the speed of movement of the joint. This muscular action may therefore be a contraction (shortening) of the muscle, controlled extension (lengthening) of the muscle, or it may in fact be an action in which force is applied within the muscle to hold a fixed position but the length of muscle does not alter. Muscular actions may be categorised as follows:

a.   *Isotonic:* The force within the muscle is overcoming the resistance but the force and speed of the contraction will vary throughout the muscle range according to the position of the limb.

b.   *Isokinetic:* The force within the muscle is overcoming the resistance but the speed of contraction of the muscle is constant throughout the full range of muscle motion.

c.   *Isometric:* The muscle force will equal the resistance opposing it to hold a position (i.e. half lever) but the muscle length will be constant.

d.   *Concentric:* The force in the muscle will overcome the resistance opposing it and the muscle is contracting (shortening), i.e. biceps in a chin-up.

e.   *Eccentric:* The force is less than the resistance and the muscle will slowly extend (lengthen), i.e. biceps extension in lowering the body from a chin-up.

10.5   Muscle groups and joint complexes

The following examples (pp. 42–46) illustrate the major muscle groups associated with various joint complexes and a knowledge of this basic anatomy and muscle function will be of value to both coach and gymnast.

A.   The shoulder girdle and shoulder joint

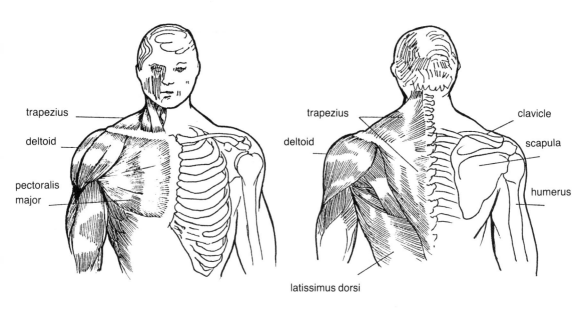

Front (anterior) view   Rear (posterior) view

Bones	*Muscles*	*Function*
Scapula (shoulder blade)	Trapezius	Rotates the scapula, pulls the shoulders backwards and downwards. Turns the head and bends the neck backwards.
Clavicle (collar bone)		
Humerus (upper arm)		
	Deltoid (posterior and anterior)	Is used in all movements of the arm.
	Pectoralis major	Pulls the arm to the side of the body, and in front of the chest from any position.
	Latissimus dorsi	Pulls the arm backwards.

B.   The elbow joint

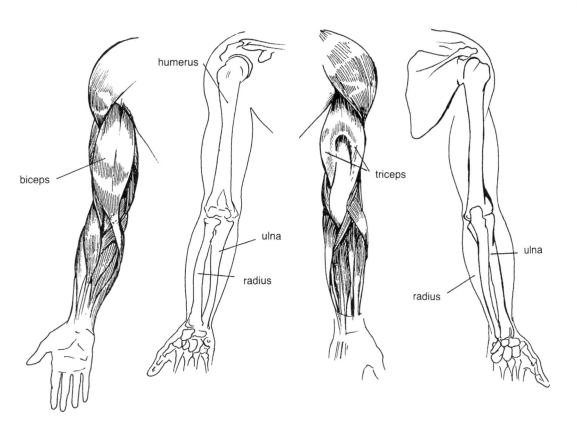

Front (anterior) view   Rear (posterior) view

Bones	*Muscles*	*Function*
Humerus (upper arm)	Biceps	Flexion of the elbow joint (chin-ups).
Radius (lower arm)		
Ulna (lower arm)	Triceps	Extension of the elbow joint (press-ups).

C.   The knee joint and ankle joint

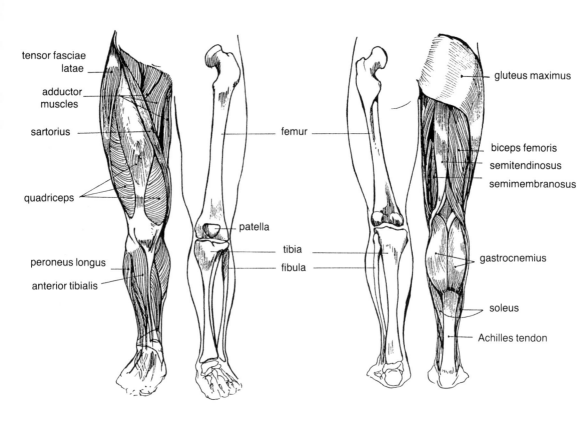

tensor fasciae latae

adductor muscles

sartorius

quadriceps

peroneus longus

anterior tibialis

femur

patella

tibia

fibula

gluteus maximus

biceps femoris

semitendinosus

semimembranosus

gastrocnemius

soleus

Achilles tendon

Front (anterior) view   Rear (posterior) view

Bones	*Muscles*	*Function*
Femur (upper leg)	Quadriceps	Extension of knee joint, i.e. straightening the leg.
Fibula (rear of lower leg)		
Tibia (front of lower leg)	Hamstrings	Flexion of knee joint (bending the leg).
Patella (knee cap)	Gastrocnemius	Plantar extension of the ankle or foot, i.e. pointing the feet.
26 bones of the feet	Peroneus longus and anterior tibialis	Dorsiflexion of ankle or foot.

D.   The hip joint

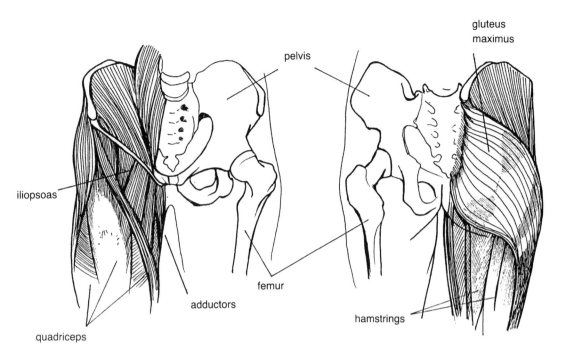

Front (anterior) view   Rear (posterior) view

Bones	*Muscles*	*Function*
Pelvis (hip girdle)	Iliopsoas (spine to femur)	Pulls the pelvis forwards.
Femur (upper leg)	Quadriceps	Lift the leg forwards (raises the femur).
	Gluteus maximus	Pulls the leg backwards.

E. The trunk

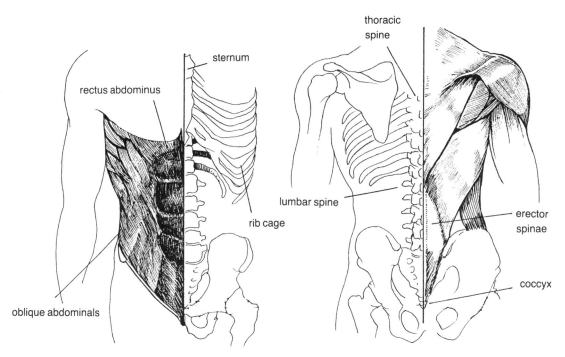

Front (anterior) view   Back (posterior) view

Bones	Muscles	Function
Vertebral column (spine) Sternum (breast bone)	Abdominals	Rounds the spine, bends forward.
Thoracic cage (rib cage)	Oblique abdominals	Twists the trunk.
	Erector spinae	Hollows or arches the spine.

In order to maintain the 'body tension' of the trunk the abdominals and iliopsoas muscles at the front of the body are contracted at the same time as the erector spinae and gluteal muscles at the rear of the body.

10.6 Diet and nutrition

Coaches will be familar with the fact that a highly tuned motor engine will not run effectively on low grade fuel. Similarly, the trained athlete also requires the correct type, quality and amount of food as fuel. Even with the right grade of fuel the engine will only fire if it is 'triggered' by a spark plug. In order for the human energy process to operate, the food intake must also contain foods which will 'spark off' the energy release process.

The study of diet and nutrition is a complex science, but it is essential that coaches, gymnasts and parents are aware of the basic principles of a good 'balanced diet'.

A.   The calorie factor

One of the most important factors relating to performance and body weight control is the intake of calories in the food we eat. Calories are burnt off with exercise and we must therefore take in the correct level of calories.

i.   If the intake of calories *exactly equals* the expenditure of calories the body weight will remain constant.

ii.   If the intake of calories is in *excess* of the expenditure the body will *gain* in weight.

iii.   If the intake of calories is *less than* the expenditure the body will *lose* weight.

It can be deduced from the above statements that the control of the calorific intake is of great importance in a gymnast's diet. Between 2,000 and 2,500 calories per day are required by a normal level of activity, but for an active young gymnast this will be raised to around 3,000–3,500 calories per day. An adult male gymnast training twice per day may need as much as 5,000–6,000 calories per day.

B.   The 'energy' foods

i.   *Carbohydrate foods*
     The energy supplied in the form of calories will come mainly from the carbohydrates; fats; and protein foods. Of these the most important source for the gymnast will be the *carbohydrate* foods such as potatoes (preferably baked), pasta, rice, bread and sugar. The carbohydrate foods release the form of stored energy necessary for dynamic gymnastic training while fats and proteins supply energy over longer periods of prolonged steady exercise.

ii.   *Vitamins and minerals*
     Vitamins and minerals are essential to the diet since they break down the energy foods to allow them to release the energy. There are a variety of vitamins, such as A, B, C, etc., and minerals (salts) such as iron, calcium, phosphorus, sodium and potassium which are essential to the balanced diet. Vitamins and minerals are obtained from such foods as cereals, fruit and vegetables.

iii.   *Protein*
     Protein is required for the building and repair of the body (i.e. muscle cells), but the amount of protein required will be adequately obtained from a normal balanced diet. A high protein diet should be avoided as this will result in excess body weight. Protein is readily available in meats but since 'red meats' contain fats it is recommended that the protein is obtained by the consumption of 'white meats' such as chicken or turkey, fish and cottage cheese.

iv.   *Fluids*
     Water is vital to the body to maintain the heat balance and to ensure efficient transport of the nutrients through the body. With exercise the body loses fluid through evaporation of sweat and we need to replace this lost fluid. This is best done by frequent drinking of small quantities of water rather than large volumes at a time. The salts lost with the sweat are adequately replaced by the normal diet and thus salt tablets are not usually required during gymnastics training.

C.   A good basic diet

The following are guidelines towards a good balanced diet:

    i.   Try to eat a variety of foods since no one food contains all the nutrients – this will provide a balanced diet.

    ii.   *Eat a good quantity of 'high fibre' foods* such as wholewheat cereals, wholewheat bread, fruit, vegetables, muesli, etc. High fibre foods are readily digested and pass quickly through the body.

    iii.   *Avoid* foods containing fat such as fatty red meat, chips, and fried foods, crisps, etc.

    iv.   *Avoid* fast foods such as those containing flavourings and preservatives with few nutrients.

    v.   *Eat a high carbohydrate diet:* baked potatoes (not fried), pasta, rice, wholewheat bread and little sugar.

    vi.   Grill foods rather than fry them – this reduces fat.

    vii.   Take in low fat, low cholesterol foods such as low fat cheese, low fat yoghurt and skimmed, not creamed, milk.

    viii.   Take in regular quantities of liquid.

    ix.   For snacks eat nuts, fruit, mixed fruit, low fat yoghurt and muesli bars – *do not* eat sugar, sweets or chocolate bars.

    x.   Eat small quantities regularly rather than huge irregular meals.

D.   The pre-competition meal

Foods such as fats and meats are slowly digested and if consumed within four hours of a training session or competition they will produce a feeling of fullness and reduce perfomance. Other foods to avoid prior to an event are greasy foods, highly seasoned foods, and gas-forming foods or drinks.

High fibre foods and carbohydrates should form the basis of the pre-training or pre-competition meal. These are readily digested, pass through the body quickly and provide the energy nutrients required for good performance.

The meals should preferably be consumed no less than two and a half hours before the event and should include such foods as fruits, cooked vegetables (not fried), wholewheat bread, fish and possibly lean white meat such as turkey or chicken. Small quantities of non-gaseous liquids may be consumed up to forty-five minutes before the event.

The consumption of large quantities of sugar (glucose) just prior to the event is not recommended as this will produce a feeling of heaviness.

11.0 The pre-session warm-up

When we participate in physical activity we utilise the neuromuscular system (the system of nerves and muscles) to control the movement of our body. When a muscle is brought into operation it expends energy. The energy is originally supplied by the blood in the form of glucose which is converted to glycogen and stored in the muscles. During muscular activity the glycogen liberates energy, leaving a residue of lactic acid. When the muscle is at rest, oxygen from the blood reduces the lactic acid into carbon dioxide and water and releases a further supply of energy in the form of glycogen. After hard physical exercise we therefore breathe very deeply in order to supply oxygen to the muscles via the blood to regain the muscular energy store.

With due consideration being given to the above information it becomes evident that the workings of the respiratory system and blood circulatory system must be efficient if we are to undergo any form of physical exercise. Since the body temperature will affect the ease with which the blood will circulate it can be appreciated that the efficiency of the muscles is directly related to body temperature. The lower the body or muscular temperature, the less efficiently the muscles work. Muscle tissue is also inflexible when cold and an increase in temperature will improve the flexibility and speed of movement of the muscle. It now becomes evident that to 'warm up' the body before any strenuous exercise is imperative in order generally to improve the efficiency of the muscles and reduce the risk of injury.

11.1 The physiological benefits of the warm-up

It is essential that a 'warm-up' period should precede all training sessions and competitions, since, if it is correctly constructed, it will provide a mental and physiological preparation and a necessary stimulus for the work to follow. If we consider the statements regarding muscles in the previous paragraph we can appreciate the physiological benefits of a thorough warm-up. These are:

    a.   The body and muscle temperature is increased, making the muscles more flexible and more efficient, since the blood supply to the muscles is improved.

    b.   The respiratory rate is increased to supply greater quantities of oxygen.

    c.   The heart rate is increased to meet the greater demand for blood circulation in order to ensure the supply of energy to the muscles.

    d.   The rate of glycogen conversion is increased to supply essential energy.

    e.   Stretching the muscle tissue, tendons and ligaments provides greater flexibility, range and speed of movement.

    f.   Since the muscles will be warm and flexible, there is less risk of muscular or other injury.

11.2 The psychological benefits of the warm-up

If the warm-up is well organised and planned it should offer certain psychological aids to the gymnast in preparation for a competition or training session. The following could be classified as psychological benefits:

a.   The emotional stress on a gymnast would be greater if he was not confident that he had suitably warmed up his muscles, etc.

b.   Having successfully completed, in the warm-up, the necessary motor skills related to the work he is to perform, he will have a psychological uplift and will therefore be less anxious and more confident in his task.

c.   If the correct motor skills are chosen they will provide a greater stimulus towards the rest of the session.

11.3   The structure of the warm-up period

A properly structured warm-up should precede all training sessions and competitions. The following will provide some guidelines for the basic warm-up.

A.   Guidelines for the warm-up

i.   There should be no time lag between the warm-up and the session or competition.

ii.   The warm-up should include exercises which warm up the whole body to ensure the necessary increase in body temperature and exercises to stretch the muscles and connective tissues (ligaments, tendons, etc.).

iii. The gym should be heated to around 21°C and the gymnasts should be suitably dressed in ample clothing to reduce loss of body heat. If these points are not adhered to, the warm-up will be prolonged or may be unsatisfactory.

iv.   The physical demand should be progressively increased throughout the warm-up but should not be such as to induce fatigue.

v.   Exercises should be selected to suit the individual gymnasts.

vi.   Exercises may include general conditioning exercises to cover areas of specific weakness and should include exercises related to the elements to be performed in the training session.

vii. The warm-up should be varied to avoid the onset of boredom; the use of music offers variety and develops a sense of rhythm.

viii. The gymnasts should be encouraged to perform the exercises correctly, with good posture and body line. This will ensure good style performance and correct technique.

B.   The three-part warm-up

The warm-up should be structured in three stages.

i.   *Preparatory warm-up*
      The aim of this section is to raise the body temperature generally and gently to stretch the muscles of the body. Exercises involving large muscle groups and the whole body should be selected and developed from a gentle pace to a vigorous exercise which may be directed to the development of strength and endurance. The types of activity to include in this section are: jogging, playing tag games, handball, volleyball and

various forms of relay type activities. This should be followed by whole body excercises and large muscle group activities, such as arm or leg circling, trunk turning, bending or twisting, head circling, wrist rolling, ankle flexing, general leg stretching and leg bending, etc. It is good practice to start at the head and move systematically through all parts of the body and to vary the exercise, to reduce the likelihood of boredom. Ballet exercises are also usefully employed to strengthen and warm up the legs, ankles, etc.

ii.   *Stretching period*
With the body now fully warmed up it is now possible safely to stretch the muscles and connective tissue to improve mobility towards the full range of the joint.

To a gymnast 'ballistic stretching' such as dynamic leg swinging has very little value and should therefore be kept to minimal use. 'Static stretching' is of much greater value and exercises may be used including 'active stretching' – where the gymnast applies his own force to stretch the muscles – and 'passive stretching' where a partner applies the '*controlled force*' to stretch the muscles. All muscle groups should be effectively stretched to prepare the gymnast for the oncoming session and reduce the risks of injuries. Please consult section 12.1 for more detail concerning specific types of stretching and stretching exercises.

iii. *Individual warm-up*
In this period the gymnast should be allowed to warm up/stretch areas of muscle groups of personal concern, such as a joint with poor range or a previously injured area. This section should also include exercises and skills which are prerequisites of, or related to, those skills to be performed in the main aspect of the session. These might include: landings, spins and turns for orientation, handstands, pirouettes and floor practices related to other apparatus skills.

11.4   The cool-down or warm-down

It is good practice to terminate the day's vigorous exercise session with a cool-down period. This involves the use of light rhythmical exercises and stretch exercises gradually to return the body to the normal state. This will allow the blood pressure to fall gradually and enable excess fluids and lactic acid to be dispersed. Without this cool-down the muscles will become stiff and sore due to fluid and lactic acid build up.

12.0 Physical preparation and conditioning

To enable any gymnast to capitalise upon any ability he may have, it is necessary for him to be mentally and physically prepared in order to facilitate the safe learning of the gymnastic skills. Without a thorough preparation he may have certain weaknesses which will not only inhibit the learning process, but may also create a dangerous situation. It is essential therefore that the basis for *all* gymnastic work is a thoroughly planned conditioning and preparation programme. The area of preparation must include such aspects as: flexibility, strength, endurance, posture, control, body awareness and spatial awareness.

12.1 Flexibility and stretching

It is desirable that all gymnasts have a good range of movement in all joints to facilitate the learning of a wide range of skills, and to allow an aesthetic expression in their performance. A limited range may prohibit the possibility of learning certain skills and may also increase the risk of injury.

Methods adopted in stretching include 'ballistic stretching' and 'static stretching'.

A. Ballistic stretching

This involves the swinging action of a limb to use the momentum of the limb to stretch the muscle. There is, however, a tendency to react at the completion of the stretch and the muscle produces a reflex action (*stretch reflex*). This reflex action tends to shorten the muscle and will cause muscle soreness. It is therefore recommended that ballistic stretching is only used as a warm-up to stretching and that it is always followed by one of the following methods of stretching.

B. Static stretching

This involves the use of slow, controlled and sustained force to improve the range in a joint complex or muscle. Once the limit of the joint or muscle has been reached the application of force is sustained for a few seconds to further stretch the muscle.

There are three forms of static stretching:

  i. *Active stretching:* The performer himself applies the force to the muscle group under stretch and sustains that force at full stretch for between 10 to 30 seconds.

  ii. *Passive stretching:* A partner applies the controlling force to the muscle group and sustains the force at full stretch for 6 to 30 seconds.

  iii. *P.N.F. stretching:* The muscle is stretched by a partner towards full range; the performer then attempts to contract the muscle under stretch and hold this contraction 6 to 10 seconds. Upon relaxation of the muscle, the muscle is further stretched and the exercise repeated.

  This form of passive stretching is *Proprioceptive Neuromuscular Facilitation* (P.N.F. stretching) and has been scientifically proven to be the most successful method of improving and maintaining range of movement.

It is essential that 'bouncing' in a stretched position be discouraged as it may lead to muscle tears and to stretch reflex shortening of the muscle.

12.2 Stretching exercises

The following are a few of the many useful stretching exercises, and though grouped under specific headings may also simultaneously stretch other muscle groups.

A. Stretching the neck muscles

Head rolling

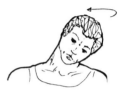

Roll the head in a full circle while keeping the shoulders still. Repeat in the opposite direction.

Resistance stretch for neck

The hands are placed on the forehead and apply a force in a backwards direction while resisting with the neck muscles. This will stretch the muscles at the front/side of the neck. If the hands are placed at the back of the head and the forward force is resisted, this will stretch and strengthen the muscles at the rear of the neck. The force may also be applied to the side of the head to stretch the muscles on the side of the neck.

B. Stretching the shoulders

Dorsal hang stretch

With the hands in overgrasp on a horizontal bar, the feet are passed through the hands and the body allowed to hang in dorsal hang position to stretch the shoulder range.

Dorsal stretch

The arms are placed behind the body, shoulder width apart, with the palms facing downwards. The body is then gently moved away from the hands to stretch the 'dorsal' aspect of the shoulder.

Seated overhead shoulder stretch

The partner extends the arms behind the shoulders. Arms should be shoulder width and back is held straight.

Overhead pull

Lying on the chest the partner draws the arms overhead with the arms parallel.

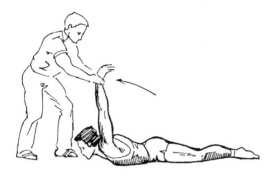

Bridge position

The partner assists under the shoulders and draws the performer's shoulders over his hands. The back must be held straight to avoid lower dorsal strain, legs and arms both straight.

It should be remembered that it is the shoulder range of muscles being stretched and relaxation and arching of the lower back detracts from the shoulders and may cause undue stress on the lower back and result in irreparable damage to the spine.

Correct bridge

Incorrect bridge

Other shoulder stretching exercises:

C.   **Stretching the trunk**

The spine will bend forwards or backwards; bend side to side; twist around the vertical axis; and circle in a trunk movement involving all these actions.

Sideways bends

The body should not bend forwards or backwards and should bend alternately from side to side.

Forwards and backwards body bends

Commence in an upright position with good posture, arch the spine backwards, return to upright, bend forwards at hips with flat back to horizontal then completely fold the body round. Return to upright with the reverse sequence.

Twisting the trunk

Keeping the body in an upright position, twist the body around the vertical axis using the arms to create turning torque.

Body circling

With the feet astride, circle the trunk to the side, forwards to touch the hands on the floor, sideways and then into back arch. Keep the legs straight at all times.

Other trunk stretching exercises:

D. Ankle, foot and lower leg stretching

The ankles and lower legs are placed under heavy loadings during take-off for tumbling and upon landing. The complex ankle joint and the Achilles tendon are particularly vulnerable and care should be taken thoroughly to warm up, stretch and strengthen these areas of the body.

Ankle circling

The legs are crossed to remove restrictions at the ankle and the foot is circulated around the ankle joint with maximum range. Repeat with the other ankle.

Front ankle stretch

From a kneeling position with the feet extended, rock backwards on to toes to stretch the foot and ankle.

Calf and Achilles tendon stretch

The stretching of the lower leg aspect may be done as follows:

i. Pressing the heel down to the floor with a straight leg from a leaning, standing position.

ii. Pressing the heel down from a front support position.

iii. Pressing the heel down further over a thick edge of a mat.

iv. In a front leaning support position with the heel pressed to the floor, attempt to hold the heel down whilst bending the knee towards the floor.

v. With the legs straight and ankles stretched (plantar flexion), draw the feet strongly up towards the knees (dorsiflexion of the ankle) to stretch the calf muscles (soleus and gastrocnemius muscles).

E. Leg stretching

Many of the exercises used to stretch the legs will simultaneously stretch not only the inner, outer, front and rear leg muscles, but will also stretch the lower back muscles (lumbar muscles). Each exercise should be held at full stretch for between 10 and 40 seconds.

Hamstring stretch

i. *Crouch-stretch:* Front crouch position, straighten legs and push the knees backwards, but maintain the hands on the floor. Gradually move the hands towards the feet each time the crouch position is used.

ii. *Body fold – standing and sitting:* The body is bent forward and the chest and face are forced into the legs.

iii. *Standing-tilt stretch:* Holding on to a wall bar, tilt the body forward to increase the force on the hamstrings.

iv. *Squat stretch:* This exercise will also stretch the adductor muscle inside the legs – use alternate legs and ease into position – don't bounce.

v. *Quadriceps stretch:* Flexible and fully stretched quadriceps muscles are essential for the execution of good front splits and overswing elements such as walk overs and handsprings. Two useful exercises are shown here.

F.   Front splits stretching

The most effective method of developing the flexibility necessary to perform the splits is to use the P.N.F. stretching principle (see p. 52) with the following exercises.

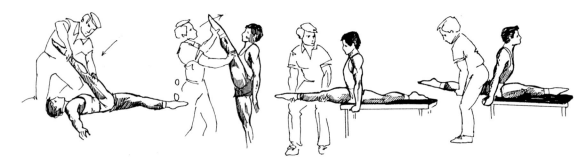

In the splits range it is necessary to stretch the hip joint, the hamstrings and the quadriceps muscles. Once the splits are achieved it can be improved and maintained using the following exercises.

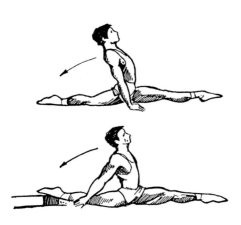

G. Side splits or box splits, stretching

This is perhaps the most difficult range for any gymnast to develop and it should be noted that the range may be limited by the restriction in the rotation of the thigh bone in the hip socket.

i. *Straddle fold:* With the legs apart to a mid range of straddle, the chest is forced between the legs – always keep the back flat – improves hip flexibility.

ii. *Knee press:* With the feet together, gently force the knees towards the floor.

iii. *Hip extensions:* Commencing in wide straddle stand, walk the hands between the legs and force the seat and chest downwards towards the floor. Then, keeping the chest low, walk the hands forwards, through low straddle stand to straddle front support, and force hips downwards to the floor. Repeat the exercise 4 to 5 times.

iv. *Straddle side fold:* Sitting in wide straddle position, fold the body sideways to place the elbow or shoulder outside the knee. Alternate to both sides.

v. *Straddle fold – Japana position:* With the legs in wide straddle, fold with a flat back to place chest towards the floor.

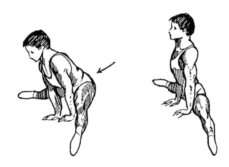

vi. *Side splits:* Front straddle stand, place the hands on the floor and gradually slide the legs apart while moving the hips in line with the feet. To achieve this position the range of movement in the hip socket, adductors and hamstring muscles must be good.

This range of movement can be further enhanced by the following exercises.

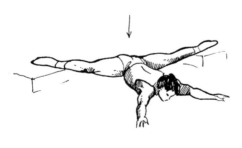

H.   Wrist stretching

The wrist is another complex joint which is often subjected to quite heavy stress and must therefore be kept flexible. Commence by clasping the fingers together and loosely roll the hands and wrists around to warm up the wrist joint. The range of movement of the wrists can now be developed by applying a controlled force in the following exercises.

Hands facing
forwards

Hands facing
backwards

Hands turned
outwards

Hands turned
inwards

Assessment of range of movement norms

DESCRIPTION	EXCELLENT	GOOD	ACCEPTABLE	POOR
1. Wrist extension	70°	90°	95°	100°
2. Elbow extension	180°	182° / 178°	175°	185°
3. Knee extension	182°	180°	178°	175°
4. Ankle extension				
5. Standing shoulder range	30°	20°	10°	0°
6. Lying shoulder range	155°	130°	120°	115°
7. Handstand shoulder flexibility	40°	50°	70°	80°
8. Bridge test (spine and legs should be straight)				
9. Elgrip hang: shoulder test	170°	160°	150°	151°
10. German or back hang: shoulder test	160°	150°	140°	141°
11. Backward arm lift: arms parallel shoulder test	80°	70°	60°	40°

DESCRIPTION	EXCELLENT	GOOD	ACCEPTABLE	POOR
12. Straddled legs body fold	2°	5°	15°	25°
13. Standing body fold: hamstring test	+15 cm	+5 cm	0 cm	−5 cm
14. Vee hold position	−2°	5°	10°	12°
15. Straddle support				
16. Quadriceps and hip test	30°	40°	55°	60°
17. Front splits	180°	178°	175°	172°
18. Side or box splits	180°	178°	175°	172°
19. Leg hold sideways	150°	130°	110°	100°
20. Leg hold forwards	130°	120°	110°	90°
21. Leg hold rearwards	45°	35°	20°	10°
22. Arabesque	85°	65°	55°	45
23. Hanging straddle (active range)	170°	155°	140°	130°

12.3 Ballet and dance training

Good posture, flexibility, co-ordination, agility, balance and strength, together with a distinct body awareness, are traits associated with both gymnastics and ballet training. Ballet and dance have become an integral part of the training and preparation programme for a gymnast and offer many benefits.

The incorporation of dance into the preparation programme will improve strength, control and body awareness, and give a better understanding of shape and posture and a greater appreciation of style and aesthetics.

A. The five foot positions for ballet

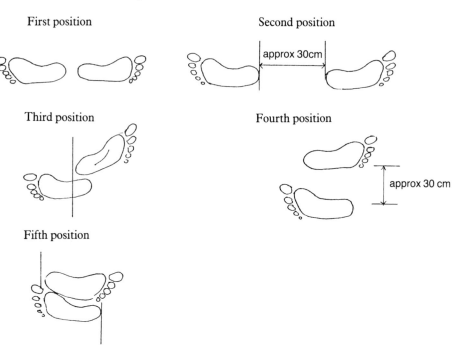

B. Transitions from one foot position to another

Assume the gymnast is standing at the 'barre', left side to the barre, left hand on the barre, right arm held in second position (see opposite).

   i. *Moving from first to second position*

      Move the weight onto the left foot and slide the right foot with pointed foot to second position.

   ii. *Moving from second to third position*

      Move the weight onto the left foot and slide the pointed right foot into third position with the heel of the right foot close to the instep of the left foot.

iii. *Moving from third to fourth position*

Move the weight onto the left foot and slide the right foot with pointed toes into fourth position.

iv. *Moving from fourth to fifth position*

Move the weight onto the left foot (back foot) and draw the right foot (front foot) backwards into fifth position, keeping the toes on the floor. It should be noted here that it is possible to move from second position to third position with the foot in third position being in front or behind the stationary foot.

When performing exercises to the front of the left leg the right foot will move from second position to third position to the front of the left foot. When performing exercises to the rear of the left leg the right foot will move from second position, to the rear of the left foot in third position.

C. The five arm positions for ballet

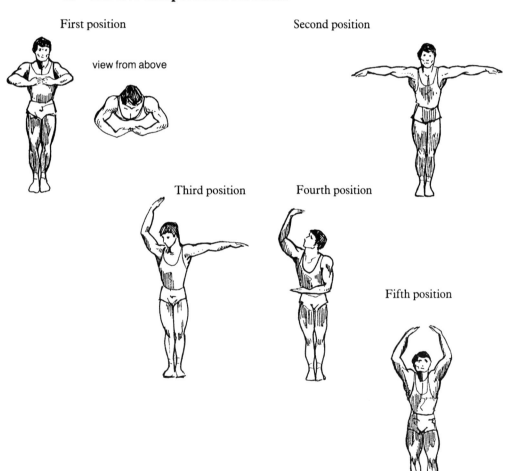

First position

view from above

Second position

Third position

Fourth position

Fifth position

D. Transition of the arms from one position to another (*port de bras*)

Generally, when *raising* the arms from one position to a higher position the *arms pass through first position*. When moving the arms from a high position to a lower position the arms are usually passed through second position.

E. Dance exercises for gymnastics training

i. *Demi plié* (half plié)

This exercise is performed with a straight spine with the 'bottom tucked in' (pelvis forward) and with the feet in any of the five positions.

Demi pliés are performed without lifting the heels from the ground and require a strong, controlled, half bend of the knees. The knees move out over the toes. It is helpful to practise the demi plié with the spine pressed flat against a wall to experience the correct posture.

This exercise is of particular benefit as it is very closely related to the ideal gymnastics landing and jumping position. It will develop the correct posture and leg strength for controlled landing and strong jumping.

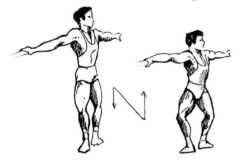

ii. *Grand plié* (full plié)

This is similar to the demi plié but is performed with a deep knee bend and in first, third and fifth position of the feet, the heels are allowed to rise off the floor.

Full or grand pliés will develop good leg strength for elevation in jumps.

iii. *Relevé*

The relevé is a rise on to the toes or, to be more precise, a rise on to the toes and ball of the foot with tension being held in the buttocks (gluteals), thighs and lower legs.

The relevé is often practised from the demi plié position and when performed in this manner it will teach the correct skill and develop the leg strength for take-off and landings. It will also establish a strong foot position upon which to perform pirouettes or other forms of turn.

iv. *Battement tendu*

Battement means 'kicking'; the term *tendu* means stretched; and if the movement is performed correctly with 'tight' legs and 'leg turn out' it will strengthen the feet and soleus muscles and give good foot and leg awareness. Turnout is where the knee is rotated outwards and the heel is turned inwards.

The battement tendu is performed from first, third or fifth position and requires the foot to slide out to the fully extended position (to 'point' the foot) and then slide back to the original position. The heel should remain in contact with the floor until the 'point' is reached and the toes should remain in contact with the floor. The foot may be taken to point at the front (*devant*) to the side (*à la seconde*) or to the rear (*derrière*). At the rear the hip must not open. An example of the use of the battement tendu is to perform the following sequence.

From third position, slide the outside foot forwards to point, close to third position, slide to the side to point, return to third, but with the foot returning to the *rear* of the supporting foot; slide to the rear point, close to rear third position, slide to the side point and close to front in third position (see figure below). This sequence of leg placements is called *en croix*.

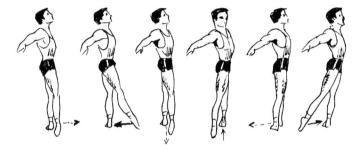

v.   *Grand battement*

In this element the leg is briskly thrown or 'kicked' to a high position, above 90°, and then closed to the original position.

The leg and foot must pass through the same pattern as the battement tendu, with the foot in point before leaving the floor and the toe returning before the heel to the floor on the downswing.

This movement is performed in first, third and fifth positions and to the front, side and rear, as with the battement tendu.

vi.   *Développé*

From first, third or fifth positions the foot of the outside leg is drawn smoothly up to the knee of the supporting leg. The knee of the working leg bends and should remain turned out. The bent leg is now straightened out to extend forward. The heel of the working leg should lead, the knee should remain turned out and the foot should not drop. The extended working leg may be held in the horizontal position for two counts before lowering with a straight leg to the original position. This exercise is repeated *en croix* (to front, to the side, to the rear) and may be performed in relevé.

vii.   *Grand rond de jamb*

In first position, with the outside working leg, degage (point the foot to the side) to second position, lift the working leg, bending the knee, to draw the toe to the knee of the supporting leg. The leg is then extended forward to the horizontal position level with the hip. The leg is then moved in a horizontal position through the side to the rear to describe a semi-circle.

The leg may now be closed from the rear to first position or it may be taken through the side to front position before closing from the front to first position.

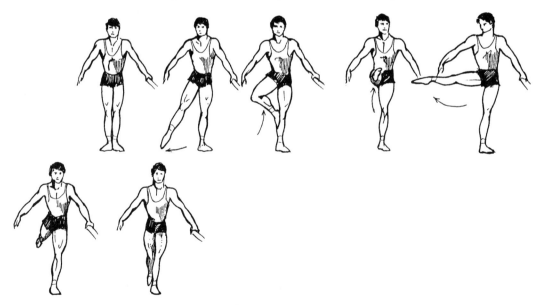

The above exercises may all be performed at the barre for a little support and the outside leg is always the working leg. Good leg tension and body posture should be maintained throughout the exercises and the exercises must be performed on each leg to develop all-round control and strength.

When turning at the barre, to change working legs, always turn *into* the barre, i.e. with left side to the barre turn inwards with a left turn and vice versa.

F.   A typical barre sequence

The following sequence must be preceded by a thorough warm-up and may be performed to a count of eight and accompanied by music at four beats to the bar.

  i. At the barre, in first position, circle outside arm, through first to second position. Bend the body forward at the hips to horizontal,·arm in second position. Fold body to knees, move arm to third position. Raise body to vertical and up onto relevé – arm in third position. Arch the back while retaining relevé. Return to upright relevé position and then lower heels to floor, arm through first to second.
  Degage to second position, and repeat the exercise in second third, fourth and fifth positions.

  ii. In first position, circle arm through first to second position. Perform *two demi pliés*, followed by *two full pliés* and then raise to *high relevé* – holding, down and then degage to second position. This excercise may be repeated in second, third, fourth and fifth positions.

 iii. In third position, circle arm to second position. *Battement tendu* twice to front, twice to side (second) closing behind on the second, twice to the rear, twice to the side, close to front. Turn to the barre and repeat on opposite leg; turn to barre again in readiness for the next exercise.

  iv. Perform two *grands battements* to the front, side, rear and side as described in (iii) above, and turn to barre and repeat on opposite leg. Turn to barre and prepare for next exercise.

   v. Commencing in first position, perform a *développé* in each of front, side, rear and side – turn to barre and repeat on opposite leg. *Note:* the elevated leg may be held for two seconds and it is also possible to raise onto relevé while holding this position. Turn to barre and prepare for the next exercise.

  vi. From first position, perform a *grand rond de jamb* from front through side to rear and return side, front to close. Then repeat from rear, side to front, and return side to rear and close. Turn to barre and repeat on opposite leg.

G.   Jumps and leaps

  i. *Chassé step*

  This step is often used to precede jumps in dance and gymnastics and consists of stepping onto one foot, closing the second foot behind the first and then stepping onto the first foot. The chassé step may also be performed with a spring from the feet to gain elevation and forward momentum.

  ii. *Sauté en première*

  This is simply a jump commencing from a demi plié in first position, springing into the air with legs stretched and toes pointed to the floor, and landing in demi plié in first position. The hands remain in low first position and good technique should be emphasised at all times. A good straight spine should be maintained and the landing sequence should be toes, ball of feet, heels, break in the ankles and knees and control with the thighs. Add to the spring a ¼, ½, ¾ or full turn.

Sauté en première   Changement

iii.   *Changement*

Commencing in fifth position, *right foot* forward, demi plié, spring into the air, extend the legs and point the feet, and changing the leg position to land in fifth position, demi plié with *left leg* forward.

iv.   *Scissor kick*

Step forward with the left leg and kick the right leg forwards and upwards. At the top of the flight of the right leg spring off the left leg and kick it forwards and upwards while dropping the right leg, to land on the right leg – step forward onto the left leg.

v.   *Push leap*

The dance terminology for a leap is a jeté.

Step onto the left leg, place the right foot behind the left foot in third position demi plié. Push off both feet extend the right leg backwards, leap onto the left foot, and close the right foot to the left foot in third position demi plié.

The inclusion of jumps and leaps into the preparation programme will ensure correct posture and technique in jumping and landing and will also develop co-ordination and body awareness.

12.4 **Postural training**

To ensure efficient and safe technique in landings, lifting and pressing, etc., it is necessary for gymnasts not only to understand good posture but also to retain that posture while performing quite complex skills. The strength aspect and greater understanding of the retention of the posture will be dealt with later. It is intended that this section will illustrate areas where young gymnasts are deficient with regard to their posture.

A.   **Standing upright**

A common enough position, but one which young children often neglect.

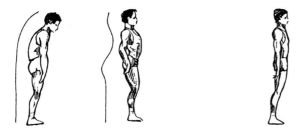

Poor posture   Good posture

Children need constantly reminding that the pelvis should be held forwards to avoid a 'hollow' in the lower back and that the shoulders are held back to create a straight spine.

B.   **Lying position**

Again, children tend to allow their pelvis to tilt backwards, particularly when raising their legs from a horizontal lying position. Teach the children first to bend their legs and press their pelvis downwards to cause the lower back to press into the floor and then stretch their legs while holding the back to the floor.

Hollow – poor posture   Flat back – good posture

Having achieved the flat back position, remind the gymnast to hold the pelvis down to retain a flat back then raise bent legs from the floor. The tendency to tilt the pelvis and arch the back must be avoided as this is a weak lifting position and will put stress on the lower back.

As the understanding improves, attempt to lift straight legs while retaining a flat back.

C.   **Leg raising**

A common error when lifting the legs during high steps or hanging lifts is to arch the lower back and tilt the pelvis backwards, similar to that described above. This produces a poor and weak lift which puts great stress on the lower back.

Poor posture   Good posture

It is again necessary to ensure that the pelvis is held forward to create a flat back and to produce a solid base against which the thigh muscles and abdominal muscles can contract to produce an efficient action.

D. Straddle stand

As with the upright stance, children often tilt their pelvis, arch their back and round their shoulders in straddle positions. To overcome this condition, teach the straddle stand with a comfortable straddle of no greater than 120°. The feet should be turned out to approx 45°, the legs straight, the pelvis forward (i.e. bottom tucked in), spine straight and shoulders back. This position is again a strong position and would be easy to maintain in the execution of such skills as a straddle vault or straddle roll.

If the legs are straddled too wide the structure of the hip and pelvic area causes the pelvis to tilt, producing a poor posture.

Poor posture   Good posture

The control of the pelvis and the ability to fix or isolate one aspect of the body to enable another to work against it is a fundamental aspect of good technique. It must be learnt thoroughly by all gymnasts and will be illustrated in section 12.7 below.

12.5 Strength, power and endurance training

Another essential element in preparation is the acquisition of a degree of strength and associated qualities which will enable a gymnast to learn the desired skills.

Physical strength is a very broad term and it will be of value to offer some basic explanation of the concepts involved. In simple terms these concepts include: muscular strength, power, endurance and body awareness.

a. *Muscular strength*

Muscular strength may be defined as the greatest amount of force that muscles can produce in a single maximum effort, i.e. the maximum load lifted in one single bar bell bench press, or the ability to hold a crucifix on rings.

b. *Power*

Muscular power is the ability of muscles to exert a near maximum force with speed. This is a very important quality in gymnastics. Examples are: i. rapid piking at the hips to raise the legs in upstarts; ii. rapid opening of the shoulder angle in backward roll to handstand.

c. *Local muscle endurance*

Local muscle endurance in the ability of the muscles to reproduce a contraction or action a number of times, or over a prolonged period before fatigue develops. This quality is particularly important in gymnastics since we must repeatedly perform a skill in training before that skill is fully learned. Lack of endurance would not permit sufficient repetition before fatigue set in.

d. *General endurance*

In order to perform exercises such as a floor exercise routine, we must develop the cardiovascular and aerobic (oxygen) or respiratory endurance to sustain the activity over a period of time. Many gymnasts fail at the end of a floor routine because their general endurance level is low.

e. *Body awareness*

It is essential that gymnasts at any level have a good understanding of their body and are able to distinguish those muscles which produce particular actions, e.g. the hamstrings flexing the lower leg and the quadriceps extending the lower leg. This understanding of the muscle actions and the ability to isolate one muscle group while moving another against it are valuable in learning gymnastics skills.

Developing strength

To improve physical strength the body must be placed in a progressive 'overload' situation in which continually greater demands are placed upon muscles. The programme for developing strength would involve the following:

i. *Improving muscular strength:* Perform a small number of repetitions of an exercise with near maximum resistance.

ii. *Improving power:* With a moderate resistance (around 60–80% max.), perform around 10 repetitions very rapidly.

iii. *Improving local muscle endurance:* With a load of 25–50% of the maximum a large number of repetitions are performed (more than 30) over a long period.

iv. *Improving general endurance:* This involves the use of whole body exercises or large muscle groups over prolonged periods. Exercises such as running or circuit training with limited rest intervals will improve general endurance.

12.6 Conditioning for gymnastics

It is the practice in gymnastics to utilise one's own body and the resistance of gravitational force to provide the resistance in conditioning training. This principle permits the exercise closely to simulate the gymnastics skill to be performed and thus strength gains and body awareness are developed simultaneously.

When designing a conditioning programme the coach should observe the following principles:

i. Only by increasing the demand by overloading will strength gains be made. However, care should be taken not to overload the body excessively.

ii. Always ensure that the correct body shape and correct technique are used and that the demand is not so great as to cause poor technique to be used.

iii. Static or hold positions will develop 'strength' and 'endurance' in muscle groups and a small number of high resistance strength skills will increase strength.

iv. Rapidly performed exercises with reasonable overload will improve 'power'.

v. A shortened lever principle will reduce the load for beginners and a longer lever may be used to increase the demand for the stronger gymnast.

Short lever – low demand   Long lever – greater demand

vi. The principle of working 'down' an incline reduces the load (i.e. sit-ups on an inclined bench with the chest above the level of the feet) while working 'up' and incline increases the load (i.e. sit-ups on an inclined bench with the feet higher than the chest.)

Down an incline – low demand   Up an incline – high demand

vii. Structure the conditioning programme to suit the needs of each gymnast and avoid using similar muscle groups in consecutive exercises.

viii. Use exercises which involve large muscle groups before those using smaller groups since the smaller muscle groups will fatigue quickly.

12.7   Conditioning exercises

The following are a selection of exercises which are essential to the preparation of a gymnast and illustrate how the demand or overload can be increased by the choice of progressive exercises.

A.   Static arch

This exercise strengthens the back and the hamstrings. Hold for periods from 10 seconds increasing to 30 seconds.

B.   Static 'dish' shape on back

This body shape together with that shown in (C) below are *essential* to the safe and successful development of a great number of gymnastics skills and the ability to retain this shape must be developed throughout the gymnast's career. Without this exercise and level of condition the gymnast will become frustrated through continued failure. *Not only does this dish shape facilitate the rapid learning of skills, but it will also provide a strong body against which other actions, such as pushing, pulling, jumping and landing can be performed.*

Unprepared gymnasts will produce a weak posture and a stressed lower back if they allow the pelvis to tilt backwards causing an arch in their lower back (see (a) below). It is essential that the pelvis is held forward in order to allow the lower back to be held flat on the floor (see (b) below).

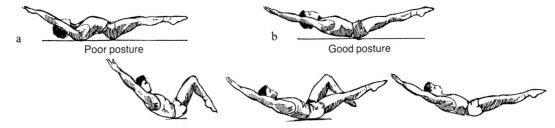

a   Poor posture   b   Good posture

The lower back should be held down onto the floor. Each attempt should be held for up to 30 seconds. The exercise will strengthen the iliopsoas, abdominal and quadriceps muscles as well as teaching good body shape.

C.   Static 'dish' shape on front

This is similar to the exercise as described in (B) above and requires a flat back, not hollow back, posture to be retained. The exercise should be held for periods increasing up to 30 seconds and will develop the strength in lower back, hamstrings, iliopsoas, abdominals and quadriceps muscles. In the more demanding positions, the shoulder strength will also be enhanced.

Poor posture   Good posture

D.   Dish shaped body raising and lowering

These exercises are progressions from those shown in (b) and (c) above and require good
control at the front and rear of the body simultaneously, to maintain the body shape.

a   b

In the two exercises shown the body must be held rigid by muscle contractions at the front of
the body (iliopsoas, abdominals, quadriceps, etc.) together with muscle contractions at the
rear of the body (erector spinae, gluteus maximus, hamstrings, etc.).

In exercise (a) the body is raised and lowered around the shoulders to simulate the up swing
and downswing at the front of an apparatus – note that in this case the *feet lead in the upwards
direction and the shoulders and back lead in the downwards direction.*

In exercise (b) the body is raised and lowered about the elbows to simulate the upswing and
downswing at the rear of an apparatus. In this case *the back and shoulders lead in the upswing
and the feet lead in the downswing.*

As the strength and body 'tension' is improved, further strengthening can be achieved by
adding force to each side at the centre of gravity as shown in (c) and (d) to provide a greater
resistance.

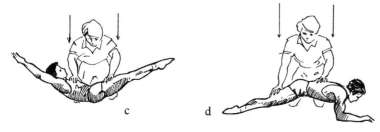

c   d

Each exercise should be held for periods increasing up to 30 seconds.

In gymnastics a great deal of time is spent in arm support and it is essential that we develop support strength and offer exercises which relate directly to swinging in arm support. The exercises below relate closely to the forward swing on side horse and parallel bars in exercise (e) and to the rearward swing on the same apparatus in exercise (f).

With improved body condition and awareness, skills moving into and out of handstand can be introduced. These skills can be designed to simulate such skills as longswing (giant swing) on horizontal bar, swing on rings and handstand rolls on floor.

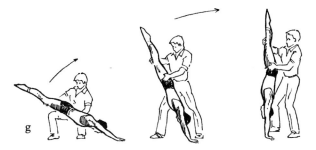

If the dish shape is held throughout exercise (g) the lift from front lying position to handstand relates to forward giant swing on horizontal bar, and the descent from handstand to lying corresponds to the swing down in a backward giant on horizotal bar and rings.

In exercise (h) the gymnast is lifted from dished position on his back to handstand with the feet leading slightly – this relates to the upward swing in a backward giant on rings and horizontal bar. The lowering from handstand to back lying position in which the back leads is closely related to the downward swing on the forward giant on rings and horizontal bar.

The importance of this dish shape and the ability to retain this shape should now be apparent. Emphasis should be continually placed on the development and retention of this shape during conditioning training and in performance of gymnastics movements. A coach could observe how often the correct placement and alignment of the pelvis and hips influences the technique involved in both learning skills and in conditioning.

E.   Abdominal strengthening

In addition to retaining a dished body shape a gymnast must frequently use actions which involve a closing of the hip angle to bring the legs to the chest or the chest to the legs. The following exercises will improve the strength of the abdominals and when the legs are held straight the quadraceps will also be strengthened. If the exercises are done with speed power will be improved and if they are performed for up to 60 seconds endurance will be improved.

The exercises are illustrated in order of difficulty and it is recommended that a gymnast progresses systematically through the exercises as shown.

Trunk lifting exercises

Leg lifting exercises

F.   Bent arm pull-up exercises

This group of exercises will develop strength predominantly in the biceps and latissimus dorsi muscles. The exercises are listed in order of recommended progression.

G.   Push-up exercises

These arm-pushing exercises should be performed with good body posture (dished as illustrated) and with the arms working in a parallel action, not turned out. Arm push-up exercises will develop strength, speed and endurance in the triceps, deltoids, latissimus dorsi and pectoral muscles.

H.   Leg strengthening

The following exercises will improve the condition of the upper and lower legs with respect to pushing, jumping and landing. It may be helpful for the gymnast to be aware of the very basic function of the leg muscles.

Extension of the ankle and heel raising contraction of the soleus and gastrocnemius muscles.

Extension of the lower leg at the knee and controlled bending of the legs when landing is the function of the quadriceps muscles.

Extension of the leg to the rear of the hip as in handspring leg drive is the function of the hamstrings and gluteal muscles.

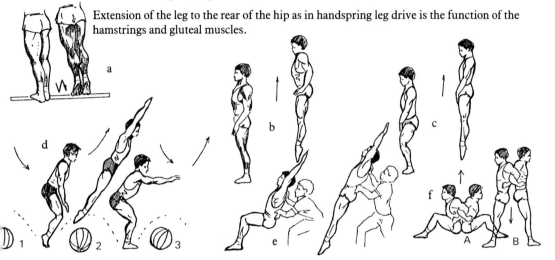

In addition to developing strength for elevation in jumping and control in landing it is necessary to develop leg strength in order to raise the limb and hold the position and line of the leg. The following exercise demonstrates this aspect of leg control but emphasis should be placed upon the retention of a flat back, pelvis forward, posture to ensure a correct technique in lifting the leg – use alternate legs for equal strengthening.

a.   Leg lift and hold

b.   Vee hold

c.   Straddle hold

d.   Seated leg lift

e.   Hang hold

f.   Single leg pusher

g.   Dorsal lifts

h.   Leg drives

I.   The use of strands for skill-related exercises

Exercises can be designed to relate closely to certain gymnastic skills with the resistance being offered by the use of an elastic material. Materials such as a bicycle inner tube, trampette elastic strand or medical rehabilitation elasticated strands are ideal for this purpose.

The degree of resistance can be varied by the choice of strand material (i.e. trampette strands offer a greater resistance than rubber inner tubes), or by the initial length of the strand (commencing with a shortened strand offers a greater resistance).

The exercises should be performed with good body posture in order to offer a good base to work against and to ensure correct simulation of the gymnastic skills. Each exercise to be repeated up to 20 times.

Exercises related to upstart and back-up skills

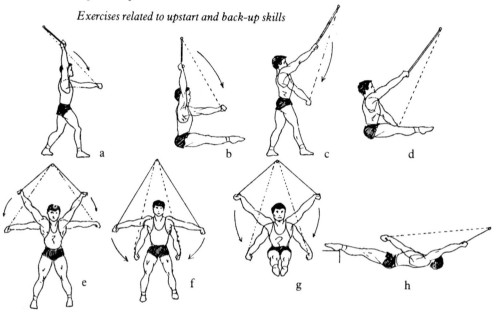

Exercise related to dislocation on rings

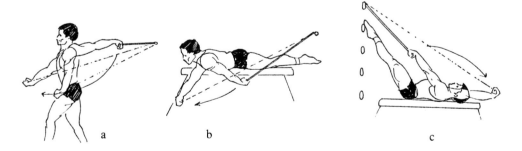

In each of these exercises the elbows should be straight and the wrists should be hyper-extended.

Exercises related to inlocation on rings

a   b   c

In these exercises the elbows are straight and the heel of the hand should lead throughout the range.

Exercises related to clear circle to handstand and backward longswing skills

a   b   c

These exercises should be performed by alternating between the back of the hand leading (for horizontal bar) and the heel of the hand leading (for rings simulation).

Exercises useful in developing other ranges related to specific skills

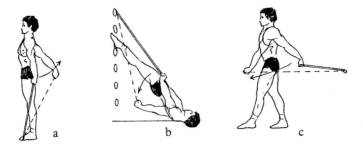

a   b   c

These exercises may be formed with the back of the hand leading or the heel of the hand leading to simulate exercises such as reverse upstart, steinerman, forward seat circle, and dislocate actions on the horizontal bar.

J.   Developing strength for lifts into handstand

The following exercises will develop the shoulders, back and hip extensor muscles to facilitate the learning of lifts to handstand.

Emphasis should be placed upon drawing the thighs into the chest with a flat lower back being retained throughout the skill. Once the inverted deep pike position with a flat back has been achieved, the legs may then be elevated to handstand with the legs initially straddled to reduce the lever.

K. Exercises to improve support strength for side horse and parallel bar skills

When performing exercises on side horse and parallel bars it is necessary to work in a high 'front support' and high 'back support' position. The following exercises will help develop both the strength and awareness required in these positions.

Front support or front planche exercises

Back support exercises

Suggested conditioning circuit for young gymnasts

CIRCUIT 'A' LEVEL 1	CIRCUIT 'B' LEVEL 2	CIRCUIT 'C' LEVEL 3
Front body hold with bent legs 20 secs.	Front body hold straight legs 25 secs.	Front body holds full extension 30 secs.
Declined push-ups 20 secs.	Inclined push-ups 20 reps.	Piked push-ups 15 reps.
Leg holds/alt. legs Front 3 × 10 secs. Side 3 × 10 secs.	Leg holds/alt. legs 3 × 15 secs.	Leg holds/alt. legs Front 3 × 20 secs. Side 3 × 10 secs.
Declined chin-ups 12 reps.	Assisted chin-ups 12 reps.	Chin-ups 12 reps.
Arched lift 3 × 30 secs.	Arched support 3 × 30 secs.	Dished front support 3 × 30 secs.
Ankle extensions 25 reps.	Demi plié jumps 30 reps.	Rebound jumps 4 × 10 jumps
Elevated lift to handstand (held) 8 × 3 secs.	Straddle lift to handstand (held) 8 × 3 secs.	Straddle support lift to handstand (held) 8 × 3 secs.
Lift to high tucked support 8 × 3 secs.	Jump to vee hold 8 × 3 secs.	Jump to Russian vee hold 8 × 3 secs.
Shoulder shrugs (dips) 20 reps.	Handstand slowly lower with straddled legs 10 reps.	Jump to tucked front planche 8 × 3 secs.

The exercises illustrated on p.83 will eventually lead to the condition necessary to hold the desired positions shown below.

Top planch   Russian hold

12.8   Typical conditioning circuit for young gymnasts

Before introducing a circuit of exercises, ensure that the gymnast has an understanding of the correct shape and technique involved in the exercises. Select exercises which meet the needs of each gymnast with respect to his age and maturation level.

Avoid using consecutive exercises which use similar muscle groups.

A well-designed circuit can be used to develop:

   i.   Strength – by increasing the load or resistance.

  ii.   Power – by reducing the time to complete a set of exercises.

 iii.   Endurance – by extending the period of exercise.

Remember to vary the exercises to maintain interest.

13.0   Body and spatial awareness

Before attempting to teach gymnastic movements, it is essential that the gymnasts have a thorough understanding and awareness of their bodies with respect to bodily tension, shape, control, landing and jumping skills and direction of twisting etc. These areas are further explained in the following sections.

13.1   Body awareness

   a.   The implementation of postural training (12.4) and ballet exercises (12.3) will enhance the general understanding of bodily tension, extension, shape and control, which are essential to the learning of gymnastic skills. The inclusion in the preparation programme of such exercises as bridge; straight, piked, tucked, dished and arched positions; together with limbs held in various positions with respect to the body, will improve the overall body awareness.

b. The gymnasts must also be made aware of the body's limitations with respect to undue stress on the spine, neck, ankle joint, wrist joint; hyperextension of the knees and elbows; too deep a flexion of the knees upon landing. This additional awareness will protect the gymnasts against unnecessary injuries.

c. It is also necessary to educate the gymnast to overcome certain instinctive reactions such as closing the eyes, allowing the body to relax, and thrusting out the arms. Such instinctive reactions could lead to increasing the risk of injury.

13.2 Safe landings and falls

The majority of injuries occur during the landing (or falling) phase of gymnastics elements and a thorough understanding of correct landing techniques and safe falling skills will reduce the frequency of injury.

A. Landing technique

A great deal of time should be spent on good take-off and landing techniques, both on the floor and from the apparatus, throughout a gymnast's career. Again, ballet training will become the basis of sound landing skills since the demi plié is adopted in all landings.

Upon contact with the landing surface the gymnast should arrive with the feet in balletic 'first position'. The toes and ball of the feet should make the initial contact, followed by an immediate and simultaneous flexion of the ankles, knees and hips. The momentum of the body is absorbed by the controlled flexion of the ankles, knees and hips, with particular emphasis on the control of the quadriceps muscles. The spine should be held straight with the pelvis tilted forward. The body should remain close to a vertical position; the knees should bend to between 90° to 120°. The heels should remain in contact with the floor until all momentum has been absorbed and the landing is completed by returning to an upright position with a straight spine and the pelvis tilted forward. When landing from flighted gymnastic movements, rotation about the *transverse axis* – as in handsprings and somersaults – is reduced by lengthening the body and raising the arms to increase inertia.

Any twisting momentum – turning around the *longitudinal axis* – should be totally eliminated prior to landing by opening out the arms to the side to increase the inertia about the longitudinal axis.

The landing

  i.   Stretch the body and arms to reduce rotation.

 ii.   The feet arrive ahead of the centre of gravity to reduce rotation and the arms are opened sideways to remove twisting and improve balance.

iii.   The forward and downward momentum are absorbed by the controlled flexion of the ankles, knees and hips.

 iv.   The upper body will move forward to further absorb momentum and maintain balance over the feet. Turning the feet out in 'first position' increases the base for balance.

  v.   When all momentum has been absorbed the body is brought to a vertical position.

The landing technique should be trained from jumps, moving forwards, backwards, with varying shapes during flight, with varying degrees of twist, and from the floor and from platforms or apparatus.

B.   Landing from falls from the apparatus

Mishaps will inevitably occur and it is therefore necessary to provide the gymnast with the skills to fall in such a way as to minimise the risk of injury. *Emphasis should be placed upon the need to spread the load upon impact over as many points of the body as possible to reduce the load taken by each point.* The following exercise may then be practised to improve the techniques deployed in fall situations.

  i.   *Fall to prone* with the fingers pointing forwards and the load being absorbed in the flexion of the wrists and bending of the elbows. Maintain a straight body to distribute further impact over the full body. The head should turn to one side.

 ii.   Jump forward from a platform and *land with forward rotation*

   a.   Continue forward into forward roll cage position with hands behind head, chin tucked into the chest, body tucked and knees apart.
   b.   Rebound jump forward into forward roll.

iii.   *Fall backwards* with the fingers pointing forwards and hands placed on floor behind the body, flex the elbows to absorb the shock and keep chin forward on the chest. Body should be slightly arched to spread further impact.

iv. Jump backwards and *land with backwards rotation* absorbing the initial impact by bending the legs, then:

    a. Place the hands behind the body, fingers forwards to allow the elbows to flex to absorb the impact and tucked backward roll out. Chin is held forwards onto the chest.

    b. Roll backwards with hands placed behind the head and roll out in a backward roll cage position.

v. *Dive forward roll* and kill the rotation by extending the body, bend the kness, hold the chin onto the chest, and bring the arms quickly to the side of the body to enable the contact to be made simultaneously with the feet, back and arms to spread the impact.

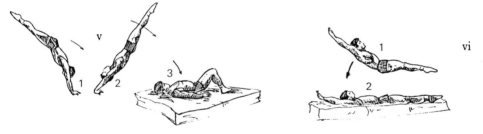

vi. *Jump backwards* with feet lifting forwards, 'kill' the rotation by raising the arms above the head, extending the back, chin on the chest and land with a flat back, arms above head and hips in a slight dish shape.

vii. *Loss of balance in handstand*: recovery can be achieved by:

    a. Tucking the head on to the chest, bending the arms and, with the body continuing to move forwards, tuck into a forward roll.

    b. Arch the feet over the head to land feet first into a bridge position.

    c. Allow the body to pivot about the hands to enable the feet to be placed upon the floor to the side of the hands.

13.3 Understanding and determining the direction of twist

A. The need to influence the direction of twist

At some point in the more advanced stages of a gymnast's development he may desire to link together elements which involve a degree of twist. Such combinations might be handspring step out into a round-off; round-off into a twisting somersault as in a Kasamatsu Vault, or twisting forward or backward somersault step out into a round-off.

In order for these combinations to be linked it is necessary for the direction of twist or turn in each skill to be related in some way.

B. The twisting rule

In simple terms the basic rules are as follows:

i.   All backward somersaults and forward somersaults should twist in the *same* direction, i.e. to the left *or* to the right.

ii. The direction of *twist* in the round-off should be *opposite* to the direction of the twists in the somersault. For example, if the favoured direction of back salto twist is to the *left*, then the round-off should be performed with a *right* twist, i.e. *left* leg leading round-off should be performed.

'twist left'   'step left'

In simple terms: *'Twist left – step left' should be the rule.*

Always consider the direction in which the chest turns as the factor determining the direction of twist.

It should now be evident that it can be advantageous if we can influence the direction of twist in gymnastics skills during the introductory stages.

C. Determining the direction of twist

The following tests usually provide quite an accurate guide to the 'natural' or 'favoured' direction of twist.

i.   Vertical jump with full turn.

ii. Jump forward and ½ turn to land on the back on to a safety mattress.

iii. Perform a full turn from front prone position.

iv. Perform a full turn from supine position (lying on the back, face upwards).

The results of the tests should be recorded and the desired direction of twist determined by consideration of:

i.   The most predominant direction of twist in the test.

ii. The coach determining which direction proved the most stable.

iii. The direction favoured by the gymnast himself.

D.   Influencing the direction of twist

Once the direction of twist has been determined by the tests listed in (c) above – assume it was to the *left – then this is the direction in which all forward and backward somersault twists should be taught.*

It may now be necessary to influence the direction of twist required in the round-off.

The rule said '*twist left – step left*': since the twist in the somersault is to be the *left* then we must encourage the round-off to be performed with the *left* leg stepping forward into the lunge – i.e. *left* leg leading.

If the attempt to influence the direction of the round-off proves to be too problematical then it may be advisable to allow the gymnast to perform the round-off in his more natural way to reduce anxiety. Unfortunately, his ability to link certain skills will be inhibited.

Once the leading leg (or thrusting leg) has been determined for the round-off then influence should be brought to guide the gymnast to lead with the same leg into kicks to handstand, handsprings and cartwheels to remove any complications.

It will also be pertinent to note that once the desired direction of somersault twist or vertical jump twist has been determined this should also be used to influence the direction of: circling on the side horse; stutz on the parallel bars; back turn on the parallel bars, etc.

Example: twisting left – then circle to the left on side horse (i.e. anti-clockwise); stutz around left arm; back turn to the left.

E.   Twisting in the inverted position

Remember that in determining the direction of the twist to the left or to the right we considered the direction in which the *chest* moved about the vertical axis, i.e. in a left twist the left shoulder moves backwards.

The same now applies when we are in an inverted position. If the gymnast were in handstand and performed a *forward pirouette* about the *left hand*, he would still be twisting to the left; similarly, in a *reverse pirouette* about the *right hand*, he is still twisting to the left.

It is important to utilise this type of skill to develop a spatial awareness of inverted direction of twist even at an early stage in a gymnast's career.

Forward pirouette
about left hand: 'left twist'

Reverse pirouette
about right hand: 'left twist'

14.0 The trampoline and rebound as aids to teaching

14.1 The benefits of the rebound facility

Rebound facilities include trampolines, trampettes or mini tramps and double mini tramps, and offer the following advantages to gymnasts:

a. An energy input to assist muscular action.
b. Greater time in the air to enable movements to be more readily completed.
c. Potentially increased rotation.
d. Less muscular effort is required from the gymnast, thus allowing a movement to be rehearsed more frequently before the onset of fatigue.
e. The greater number of repetitions speeds up the familiarisation of the movement and learning is accelerated.
f. A wide range of skills closely related to gymnastics movements can be taught.
g. Spatial awareness is greatly enhanced, thus giving a greater awareness of one's position and shape during gymnastics elements.

14.2 Safety and the use of rebound facilities

Prior to commencing a session of rebound it is important to implement the following safety inspection schedule.

i. Check that the trampoline is correctly assembled with all braces secure, that springs are correctly fitted and safety pads in position.

ii. Check for sufficient headroom and that the area around and beneath the trampoline is free from obstruction.

iii. The gymnasts and coaches should be trained in the correct assembly and dismantling of the trampette and never allow the assembly or dismantling without supervision.

During a rebound session it is essential that the following safety recommendations are adhered to:

i. A gymnast must only work under the supervision of a trained coach.

ii. A minimum of four trained 'spotters' should always be in attendance and positioned one at each end and one at each side.

iii. Correct gymnastic clothing should be worn together with non-slip gym slippers or socks. Do not permit bare feet on webbed trampoline beds.

iv. Safety mattresses may be used at the end of the trampoline but they must be effectively placed.

v. Allow only one performer at a time to work on the trampoline.

vi. Never allow a performer to jump down to dismount from the trampoline since injury can result by landing on a non-resilient surface following the work on a highly resilient bed.

vii.   Ensure that the performers always work within their capabilities and never 'out-jump' themselves.

viii. Remember that performance will diminish as the gymnast becomes tired and accidents may occur. Limit the duration of each period to suit the level of performer.

After the session supervise the folding away of the trampoline in the following manner:

i.   Fold one end of the trampoline whilst the braces of the other end are still in place and lower the frame gently onto the main frame.

ii.   Fold the second end onto the main frame.

iii. Carefully raise one end of the frame and fit the wheel stands securely into place.

iv.   Tilt the frame, ensuring that the second end to be folded hangs down to hold the first end into position and that the bed is securely clamped to the wheel frame.

v.   Carefully wheel the trampoline, store it and secure it with a lock and chain.

14.3   Teaching basic trampoline skills

The use of the rebound facility is a great asset to all levels of gymnastics training, but it is necessary for the gymnast to have a thorough understanding of the basic core trampoline skills. Once these are effectively learnt they can be the foundation upon which a wide variety of skills can be developed.

A.   Jumping and landing

i.   *Jumping*

If, upon impact with the bed, the body and legs are held in tension, then the gymnast will receive the effect of the resilience of the bed and elevation and/or rotation will be gained.

ii.   *Stopping*

However, if upon contact with the bed, the body is allowed to flex to absorb the reaction, then the bounce from the bed can be 'killed'.

Hence, if we need to gain height or rotation the body must have tension and when we wish to stop a bounce we must absorb the bounce by a controlled bending of the body at the knees, ankles and hips. Thus to stop the bounce during a landing we again use a controlled demi plié position.

Jumping with 'tension'   Stopping with 'flexion'

iii.   *Types of jump*

Once the basic jumping and landing skills have been learnt the shape within the flight phase can be varied to include tucked, piked, star and straddled piked positions.

iv.   *Including a twist in the jump*

The twist in trampoline-rebound situations can be created by:

a.   *Torque turning:* Pushing against the bed with the feet or the hands in the opposite direction to the desired direction of twist; i.e. pushing with the toes or feet to the *right* causes a reaction which results in a twist to the *left*.

b.   *Tilt twisting:* By raising one arm and/or dropping one arm an eccentric displacement is made upon the body and the body will twist.

   i.   *Tilt lifting the left arm:* the body will rotate towards the raised arm and will therefore turn to the left.

   ii.   *Tilt dropping the right arm:* will cause the body to turn to the left.

c.   *Two-axis twisting – cat twist:* By moving the lower body in the opposite direction to the upper body the body alignment is taken away from the single long axis and a two-axis twist will result – i.e. cat twist.

a.   Torque twisting   b.   Tilt twisting   c.   Cat twisting

Invariably, when twists are created in gymnastics and trampolining, a combination of two or more of the twist actions are combined to create the twist. It is essential that the performer becomes proficient in all three techniques.

The twisting actions should be first introduced to straight body jumps and should follow the progression of ½ turn, full turn, and 1½ turn with the preparatory jump turns being initially mastered on the floor.

B.   The seat drop

Introduce this skill from a stationary standing position with arms at the side of the body, bend the knees to depress the bed and give a slight upthrust, raise the legs forward to a piked position and 'seat drop' to land on the bed, arms to the side, fingers pointing forwards. It should be possible to press down on the bed with the hands during the seated position to gain a lift from the bed. The arms are then raised during the flight and the legs are snapped down beneath the body to stand on the bed. The seat drop can then be performed from an elevated jump using a similar technique.

The seat drop to stand

The seat drop half twist to seat drop – torque turning from the hands against the bed initiates the twist which can then be assisted by a tilt turn or cat twist action.

C.   The front drop

The front drop should be developed by means of the following progressions.

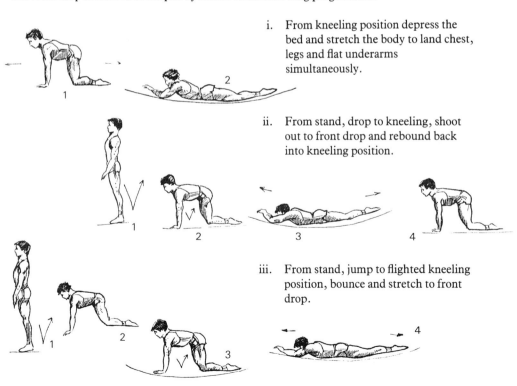

i.   From kneeling position depress the bed and stretch the body to land chest, legs and flat underarms simultaneously.

ii.   From stand, drop to kneeling, shoot out to front drop and rebound back into kneeling position.

iii.   From stand, jump to flighted kneeling position, bounce and stretch to front drop.

iv.   From bounce raise the hips and lift the
feet rearwards to front drop.

Once effectively mastered, the front drop should be taught to elevate the shoulders, and
'kick in' the feet during the flight from the front drop, to land in standing position.

D.   The back drop

The following sequence is recommended for the development of the back drop.

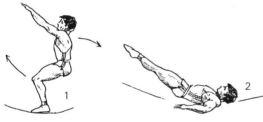

i.   From sitting position allow the
shoulders to drop backwards, lift the
feet forwards to a deep dish shape and
land upon a flat back simultaneously
with the underarms contacting the
bed. Look for the feet during the back
drop to 'clear' the head.

ii.   Elevate the hips and chest during the
flight then lift the legs into a dish prior
to the back drop landing upon the bed.

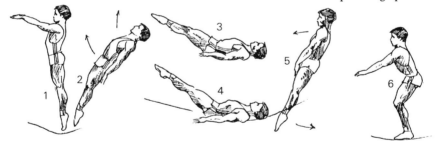

Once a bounce can be achieved from the 'back drop' the shoulders can be brought forward
and the heels snapped down to stand.

E.   Combination of skills

When each of the aforementioned skills are competently performed individually they may be
linked together to form combinations such as:

Front drop to back drop; front drop half twist stand.
Seat drop to front drop; front drop to seat drop.
Back drop to front drop; back drop half turn to stand.
Seat drop half twist to seat drop; half twist to front drop.

14.4 Further uses for the trampoline

The trampoline can be gainfully employed in the teaching of other skills as shown below.

a. *Teaching the back flip*

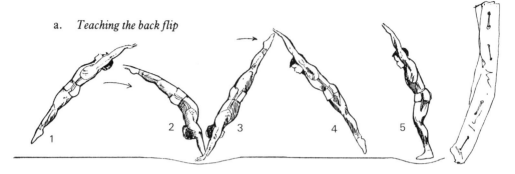

b. *Clear circle to handstand*

Holding strands, deep fold. Press out towards handstand.

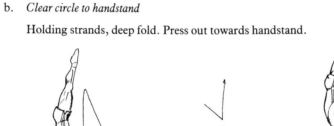

c. *The handspring vault*

Using the trampoline, covered with safety mattress and agility mattress, as landing area.

d. *The teaching of the forward longswing*

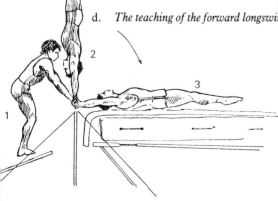

14.5   The use of the trampette

The trampette is a useful training aid if correctly used, but can be very dangerous if irrationally used or used without supervision. Control in flight to eliminate over-rotation, the execution of correct landings, and safe recovery from falls must always be the dominant factors. It is essential that the trampette springs or strands are covered with a full, purpose made, safety pad and that a good landing surface comprising a bed of safety mattresses covered with agility mattresses is used. Always use a landing surface of adequate area and check frequently for gaps between the mats.

A.   The recommended trampette situations

i.   *Running forward take-offs*

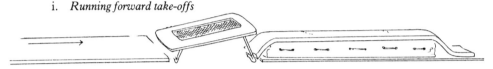

It is recommended that a 'spotter' is in attendance at the above situation at all times.

The above forward-moving situation is useful for the teaching of forward take-off jumps, including straight, tucked, star, piked, ½ turn, full twist, together with such skills as front somersaults.

ii.   *Forward skills from an elevated platform*

The gymnast must avoid excessive forward lean upon take-off.

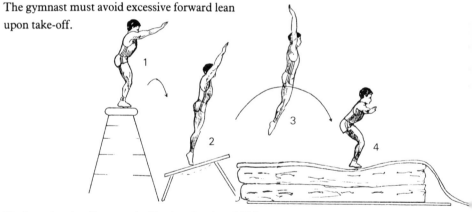

iii.   *Platform situation* (for round-off or handspring skills)

This situation is useful for introducing round-off backward take-offs in readiness for the performance of backward somersaults.

Care must be taken to avoid over-rotation.

iv.   *Snap-down situations*

The snap-down action from a round-off or back flip can be simulated in this situation. Familiarisation with this set-up will enable the gymnast to perform backward somersaults or similar skills, at a later date.

A variety of jumps, such as straight, star, tucked, ½ twist and full twist can be performed in the above rebound situations.

14.6   The double mini trampette

The double mini trampette can be used for forward running, backward moving, or round-off type take-offs with skills being incorporated as described for the ordinary trampette.

14.7   Summary

Rebound situations, while offering many benefits to the gymnast and coach, are potentially dangerous situations if not correctly controlled.

Ensure that:

i.   A safe apparatus set-up is used and frequently checked.

ii.   Clear instructions are given.

iii. Adequate spotters of suitable experience are used.

iv.   Gymnasts only work to the level their ability and experience allow.

v.   Logical skill progressions are used; only progress when competence is clearly displayed.

15.0 The teaching of gymnastics elements

Before entering into the teaching of specific gymnastics elements as illustrated in sections 16.0 onwards, it may be pertinent to reflect upon the recommended good teaching and coaching guidelines.

i.   Select those exercises which are suitable for each individual gymnast with due regard to his age, size, ability and experience. Ref: Section 7.2 d.

ii. Carefully select bodily awareness and conditioning exercises which relate to the skill being taught. Ref: Sections 12.0 and 13.0 and particular skill developments in the later text.

iii. Select suitable progressive skills and ensure they are fully understood before progressing. Ref: Sections 7.2 d and Sections 16.0 onwards.

iv. Introduce a new skill by means of a visual aid (film, picture, video or live performance) and discuss its development and the technique with the gymnast prior to commencing the programme of related skills. Ref: Section 7.2c.

v.   Always err on the side of safety; structure a good safe environment; ensure adequate spotting or assistance; and if in doubt seek guidance from a more experienced coach. Ref: Section 4.0.

vi. When teaching elements involving twisting or turning around the long axis of the body encourage the same direction of turn in all skills. Ref: Section 13.3.

16.0 Floor elements

16.1 The handstand

The handstand is an element and shape which is fundamental to gymnastic development and should be frequently practised by gymnasts of all levels.

A. The handstand technique

1   2   3   4   5   6

i.   Body fully stretched, raise lead leg in front of body. N.B. the lead leg should coincide with the lead leg for a handspring, round-off or cartwheel.

ii.   Make a deep lunge, the body pivoting around the lead leg.

iii.   Close the chest to the thigh of the lead leg but retain the 'open' angle in the shoulders. This will ensure the correct placement of the hands in front of the leading foot.

iv.   The kick to handstand phase should be a controlled swinging action in which the shoulders move marginally in front of the hands to offer a degree of balance. The upper back should lead into the handstand position, followed in sequence by the lower back, seat and lastly the legs. This will ensure that a dished shape is maintained throughout the swing.

v.   As the upper body and seat arrive in the vertical position the shoulders are brought backwards in line with the hands by thrusting the arms.

vi.   The body is then held in a straight line to slightly dished shape and the balance maintained by forces through the hands and control at the shoulders.

If the handstand is taught in the manner prescribed above it will be easy to relate this technique at a later stage to: swing to handstand on parallel bars; longswing forwards on horizontal bar; and swing forwards to handstand on rings.

B.   Supporting the gymnast

i.   Beginner:
shoulder and hips

ii.   Intermediate stage:
hips and abdomen

iii.   Advanced stage:
hips only

C.   Orientation skills

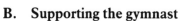

Body posture and tension

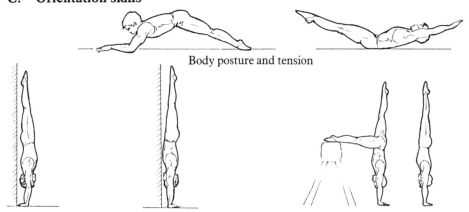

Back to the wall   Front to the wall   Leg lever to handstand

16.2 Backward roll to handstand

It is possible to perform the roll to handstand with bent arms or with straight arms. The bent arm method relates to the backward roll to handstand on parallel bars while the more contemporary straight arm method is closely related to the clear circle to handstand on horizontal bar, the circle to handstand backwards on rings and undersomersault on parallel bars.

In both cases it is essential that the dished body shape is maintained throughout the upperward press to handstand. It is quite common for young gymnasts to lose body tension when the pressing phase is commenced. This should be discouraged and the dished body shape reinforced at all times.

A.   Introducing the backward roll to handstand

i.   Down an incline: ii.   Supporting
     'see the feet and press'

iii.   Straight arm press: note the position of
       the hands

B.   The straight arm backward roll to handstand

During the initial roll fold the body deeply and reach as far back as is comfortably possible with the hands. As the seat touches the floor, rapidly move the arms overhead in readiness for the press. Retain a body fold until the feet are above the shoulders (i.e. see the feet) and then quickly open out the shoulder angle to press the body to handstand.

16.3 **The cartwheel**

A. **The technique**

Commence facing forwards and lunge as for a handstand but place both hands at 90° on a line in front of the lead leg. Swing the leg strongly through sideways straddle handstand. Place the first leg close to the second hand and as the trunk is brought upright to stand press strongly with the first leg on the floor and elevate the second leg.

B. **Introductory skills**

i.   The ending   ii.   The ending   iii.   Down an incline
                                from support

'6.4 **The round-off**

A. **The technique**

The round-off is best described as a cartwheel with a quarter turn inward during the flight from the hands.

The foot and hand
placements

During the transfer from the lunge position (1) to position at (2) the chest should 'drive' downwards towards the floor to aid the powerful upswing of the second leg. A strong thrust from the arms is added at (3) as the body shape is quickly changed to a 'dish'. During the flight from the hands the shoulders should be elevated as the feet are brought quickly to the floor.

Note: It should be noted at this point that the position of the body following the round-off should be adjusted to suit the element to follow it.

   i.   For a back flip the feet are brought close to the hands to cause the upper body to rotate quickly backwards.

   ii. For a back somersault or an element requiring flight the feet are pushed away from the hands to create a flatter flight from the hands in readiness for the strike from the feet (see below).

   i.   Round-off for a back flip   ii. Round-off for a flighted jump

B.   Introductory skill progressions

   i.   The *'snap up'* of the upper body

A common fault in the round-off is to pike the legs down to the floor from the handstand position, resulting in a finishing position which inhibits the execrution of any further elements. If a good snap up of the upper body is taught in the initial stages this should remove the likelihood of the pike down occurring. The correct finishing shape will therefore be produced from the outset and hence good technique will be ensured.

Support with the left hand across the front of the deltoid and armpit and elevate the shoulders with this hand, and use the right hand around the waist to act as the point of pivot. The feet are snapped downwards into a dished shape followed by a push from the arms to elevate the shoulders. This will produce good rotation about the feet upon contact with the floor.

ii.   The cartwheel with ¼ turn inwards

Teach this skill from an elevated platform to establish flight from the hands and develop a dish shape in the body upon thrusting from the hands.

Emphasise the use of the 'snap up' action shown in (i) above.

iii.   *Developing legswing* and creating flight from the hands

If the gymnast performs the round-off up an inclined platform as shown below this will encourage the gymnast to improve the legswing and leg push while maintaining the flight and shape during the snap up.

16.5   The back flip

Useful prerequisites to learning the back flip are: the ability to perform a good 'snap up' action as described for the round-off as this will avoid the complication of a poor exit from the flip; and good shoulder flexibility to allow a good reach back with the arms in the flight onto the hands.

A. The back flip technique: standing back flip

The back flip should commence by first displacing the body backwards off balance at (1) followed immediately by sitting to a knee bend of around 120° with a simultaneous downswing of the arms (2). *The heels must be down at all times and there must be no forward lean of the body. The knees must also remain behind the line of the toes at all times.*

The body continues to rotate backwards and a strong armswing is introduced to lead the body into the first flight phase. A powerful straightening of the legs adds rotation and backward thrust to create the desired long and low flight onto the hands (3) and (4).

The angle in the shoulder joint will close slightly as the body changes from a hollow to dished shape to initiate the snap up from the hands (5). The thrust from the arms adds to the flight and rotation to enable the snap up to occur with a high but short flight onto the feet (6) and (7). The arms should continue to rise during the flight from the hands to the feet.

B.   Do's and don'ts for back flips

i.   *Do not* allow the body to bend forward, the heels to lift off the floor or the knees to travel in front of the feet during the first phase of the flip – this will cause too much elevation and insufficient rotation.

ii.   Ensure that the hands are positioned between *parallel* and *turned inwards upon contact with the floor*.

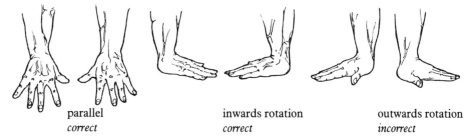

parallel   inwards rotation   outwards rotation
correct   *correct*   *incorrect*

C.   Skill progressions

i.   A good strong snap up from the hands to the feet.

ii.   Slowly handle the gymnast through the sequence of movements to teach the order and shape of the element – do not permit drive at this stage. Handle as shown below in (a). From handstand transfer the support to method (b) and enable the gymnast to execute a good snap up.

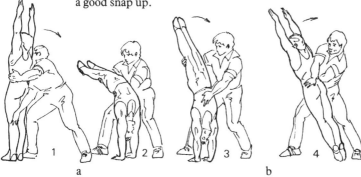

1   2   3   4

a   b

iii.   Encourage a strong arm drive backwards and co-ordinated leg push. Support as illustrated to resist back thrust.

iv.   Combine the arm drive and leg thrust with the shaping developed earlier and complete the backflip. Support as shown in (iia) above.

v.   Commencing the flip from a slight incline will encourage backwards momentum.

16.6   The round-off back flip

Having learnt the round-off, the back flip and the snap up from handstand, the following progressions can be used to introduce the round-off back flip combination.

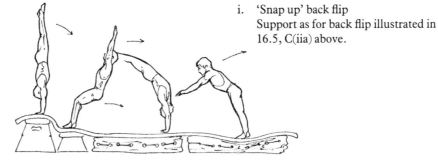

i.   'Snap up' back flip
Support as for back flip illustrated in 16.5, C(iia) above.

ii.   Perform the round-off back flip following numerous successful attempts at the skill above.

Support the gymnast in the back flip only in the usual manner but ensure that you make contact with the gymnast as early as possible upon completion of the round-off.

If the two elements have been properly learnt it is often found that the momentum gained from the round-off allows easier performance of the back flip.

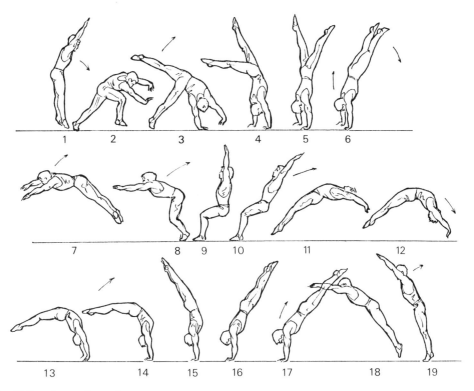

16.7 The handspring

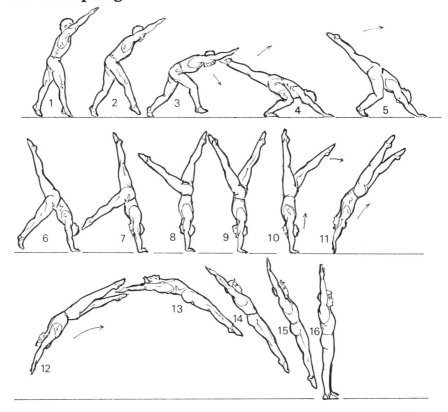

A.   The technique

The shoulder angle should be held fully open and the chest driven down towards the thigh of the bent leg into the lunge position.

The rear leg commences the powerful drive as the chest drops towards the thigh. As the driving leg approaches a straight line position with the body the bent leg now straightens rapidly to add to the rotation about the hands. The legs continue their driving action right through the vertical position and do not, in fact, come together until just before landing. A strong arm thrust is added, from a small arm bend and shoulder push just before the handstand, to create the necessary elevation for flight onto the feet.

The head should be held in a neutral position throughout.

B.   Skill progressions

i.   *Development of shape*

Kick through the handstand position to a hollow back position with the arms vertical, with the assistance of a supporter.

i   iia   iib   iic

ii.   *Leg drive and arm thrust*

The coach supporting, left hand under the gymnast's right shoulder cupping the deltoid and with the right hand around the abdomen, the gymnast rehearses the powerful leg drive and co-ordinated arm push.

iii.   *The handspring from a raised platform*

Supported in the same manner as described in (ii) above, the gymnast performs a handspring from an elevated platform. This provides flight from the hands to enable the gymnast to experience the required flight. Take care to prevent over-rotation upon landing. This can be prevented by retaining the support on the arm or shoulder upon landing.

iii

iv. *The handspring at floor level*

Following numerous successful attempts at the skill shown in (iii) with minimal assistance being required, the gymnast may then perform the handspring on the floor mats with assistance being offered initially in the same manner as described in (ii) and (iii) above. To improve rotation, the handspring may now be preceded by a strong skip-up action as illustrated. At this stage it is possible to offer assistance around the waist only (the point of rotation).

iv

C. The handspring step out

Once the handspring is being performed competently progress can be made to step out of the handspring.

First orientate the gymnast regarding the desired split of legs and the leg to become the landing leg.

If the right leg steps into the lunge (right leg stepping handspring) then it is the driving left leg that becomes the landing leg. This enables the gymnast to land on the left leg and step into the lunge on the right leg for successive handsprings or round-offs.

Support around the waist as shown in (iv) above during the initial attempts.

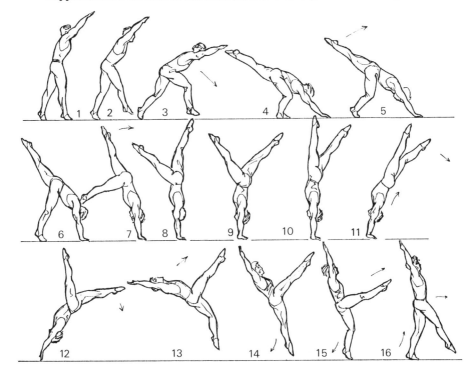

16.8 The dive forward roll

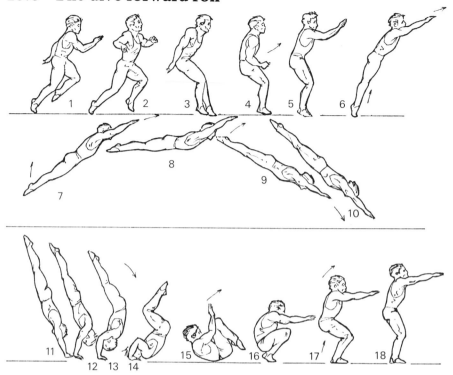

A. The technique

During the jump preceding take-off the feet should glide in front of the body and the arms should drive from a rearward position into a forward upswing. The body will swing about the feet and the arms continue to drive forwards and upwards. With the upper body just in front of the feet a powerful push is added from the legs to produce both flight and rotation about the C of G. Since the rotational requirement is small, the arms and body are held at full stretch to control rotation and the head is held in a neutral position. Upon contact with the hands on the floor the head is 'tucked' in, the angle in the shoulders begins to close, and a controlled bending of the arms lowers the shoulders on to the floor. The knees and hips may then be brought into the tucked position to complete the roll.

B. Progressive skills

i. It is imperative that a complete command of forward roll and handstand forward roll is established prior to learning the dive roll.

ii. Perform, with support, a dive towards handstand and roll onto an elevated platform of safety landing mats.

iii.   Perform the dive roll as described above with support but onto a single safety mat. Still maintain the same height on flight path.

iv.   Finally perform the drive roll onto suitably padded tumbling/floor mats with progressively reducing support as the awareness improves.

16.9   The headspring

The headspring is classified as an overswing skill which can be developed simultaneously as a floor skill or a vault.

A.   The technique

Commencing from a crouch position, reach forwards with the hands and place the forehead on the floor between and in line with the hands. As the arms reach forwards the legs are rapidly straightened to give a low trajectory on to the hands.

The now straight legs are held low until the seat moves across the hands into an off-balance position. At this point the legs are driven strongly into an arched body shape to add to the rotation. The strong arm push is added, to give flight, once the body has rotated beyond the vertical position.

Upon landing on the feet the arms and shoulders are brought upright with the assistance of a strong abdominal contraction.

B.   Progressive skills

i.   From crouch, jump forwards into piked headstand position with the feet remaining low and the seat moving off-balance over the hands.

ii. From the skill shown in (i) when the body is off-balance the legs can be driven strongly
and the arm push added to establish the action and timing involved in this skill.
Support at the hips to draw the body off-balance and lift the body to rest with the legs
across the supporter's shoulders.

iii. Once the skill illustrated in (ii) is performed correctly with a strong leg drive and arm
push the gymnast may be assisted through the full headspring from the platform.
Assist by supporting with the nearest hand under the shoulder (deltoid) and the second
hand around the waist to pull the body off balance. The hand on the shoulder assists
with the flight and prevents over-rotation upon landing. The hand around the waist
becomes the pivot about which the body rotates and also supports the lower back and
thighs during flight and landing.

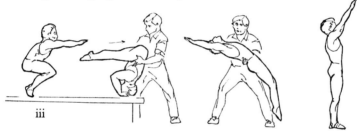

iv. The headspring may now be taken to floor level as a floor skill or to vault.

Note: good hip flexibility will enable the feet to be driven under the body to simplify the
landing phase.

16.10 The flyspring

A. The technique

From the run the feet are taken ahead of the body as the arms are taken behind the body.
The arms are then driven forward and downwards towards the floor to develop a low flight
path. The strong leg thrust is added to the forward leaning body to create rapid forward
displacement of the hips. As the hips pass over the line of the hands the legs strike strongly

to produce rapid rotation, to which the arm thrust is then added. During the flight from the hands the legs are driven beneath the body to enable the shoulders to be brought quickly to an upright position.

B. Progressive skills

i.   From a couple of paces, double foot take-off into piked handstand. The leg drive should force the hips across the hands and the body should move off balance. Coach to support at the waist.

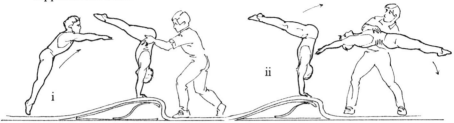

ii.   Following on from exercise (i) the gymnast drives the legs into an arched body shape and adds the arm thrust to complete the flyspring. The element should be performed as a rotational rather than flighted skill.

iii.   The flyspring may be rehearsed from a rebound situation as shown below.

iv.   The element may now be transferred to floor with the emphasis being placed upon a low flight, rapid leg drive and strong arm thrust.

17.0 Side horse – pommel horse

17.1 Preparatory conditioning skills for pendulum swing

The essential features of good pendulum swing are good support strength, good leg strength, the ability to transfer the weight from one hand to the other in co-ordination with the leg swings; and good hip flexibility. (Refer to section 12.2 f/g for suitable conditioning exercises.)

The following skills will help to develop an understanding of pendulum swings and improve his ability to perform them.

Each of the above exercises should be held for a minimum of five seconds with between 5 and 8 repetitions on *each* leg being attempted.

The exercises above are useful for developing transference of weight and support strength, and involve hand walking and rocking on the apparatus.

17.2 Pendulum swing in front support

A.   The technique

A high shoulder support is essential to all good side horse swings and this must be retained throughout the swing.

In the front support pendulum swing the upper leg should be *swung upwards towards a vertical position but should remain behind the line of the shoulders*, i.e. the leg swings upwards and slightly away from the horse. The bodyweight should be moved away from the upper leg to lean onto the support arm and the other arm can be raised from the handle. The lower leg should also drive upwards in unison with the lead leg and should reach a horizontal line through the elbow of the support arm. A swing of equal amplitude should be achieved at both sides of the swing.

B.   **Introductory skills**

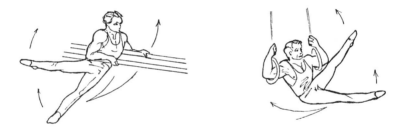

C.   **Supporting the pendulum swing in front support**

17.3 Pendulum swing in back support

A. The technique

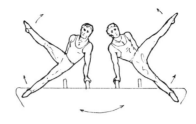

The upper or lead leg should be swung upwards and *in front of the shoulder*, i.e. forwards away from the horse, while the lower leg should swing in unison to above the line of the horse. A strong shoulder lean away from the direction of the lead leg should accompany the swing to displace the weight over the support arm. An attempt should be made to clear the horse with both legs to develop a free swinging action.

B. Supporting the pendulum swing in back support

17.4 Pendulum swing in straddle support

A. The technique

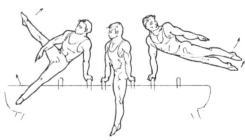

In the diagram above the gymnast is astride the horse with the *left leg in front* of the horse and right leg to the rear of the horse. It will help to think of the *left leg being in back support position* and the right leg in front support position.

When swinging towards the right with the right leg being the dominant leg, it should be swung upwards and *behind* the shoulder (as in front support pendulum swing). When swinging towards the left, the left leg is the dominant leg and it should be swung upwards, in front of the left shoulder (as in back support pendulum swing).

The shoulders must lean in the opposite direction to the swing to transfer the support and an attempt should be made to establish a good rhythm in the swing.

During the straddle pendulum swing the hips will take a slight diagonal alignment with the horse.

17.5 Front shears

A. The technique (front shears right)

From pendulum swing in front support the left leg is swung upwards behind the left shoulder then across the horse to create a straddled pendulum swing. As the legs swing to the right the weight is transferred on to the left arm and the right leg swings *upwards and behind the right shoulder*. The left leg is taken backwards across the horse (i.e. undercuts) and then the right leg is allowed to cross the horse to commence the downward swing in front of the horse. The shear to the left is a similar pattern but the left leg is the dominant leg, lifting upwards and behind the left shoulder.

B. Sequence for developing the front shear

The sequence of skills shown below will be of great value in developing good technique and thorough understanding of the front shear on side horse.

Assume a shear to the *right* is being learnt.

  i. *Pendulum swings*

    Amplitude in pendulum swing in front support; back support and straddle support.

  ii. *False shear*

    From front support, swing the left leg upwards to the left to cross the horse and swing in straddle support to the right. The right leg now becomes the dominant leg and swings upwards behind the right shoulder. The left leg 'undercuts' to the back of the horse and under the right leg. Both legs then swing downwards in straddle front support position to repeat the skill. Rehearse this exercise until it can be fluently repeated three times consecutively.

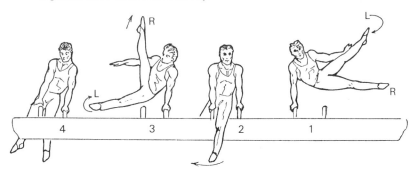

iii.   *Front shear*
First perform a rhythmical 'false shear' as described above. Swing the left leg in front of the horse into straddle swing and continue to swing right to perform the front shear right with a smiliar pattern and timing as the false shear.

iv.   Repeat the above sequence for a front shear left.

v.   Perform the following sequence without breaks: false shear right, front shear right, false shear left, front shear left.

vi.   Then practice consecutive front shears, right and left.

17.6   Backward shears

A.   The technique (back shears to the right)

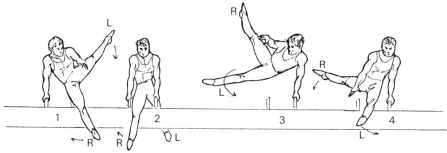

During the swing from left to right the right leg becomes the dominant leg and it is swung forwards and upwards in front of the horse. The weight of the body is transferred onto the left arm to permit the upswing to occur and to enable the right arm to be removed from the handle.

Towards the top of the swing the right leg is momentarily held in front of the horse while the left leg is circled under the right leg, from the back to the front of the horse. The left hip is then pushed forward, the right leg is taken to the rear of the horse and the downswing commences. The right hand is replaced on the handle and the left leg becomes the dominant leg in the swing towards a back shear left.

B.   The sequence for developing backward shears

Assume a shear to the *right* is being taught.

i.   Correct technique and good amplitude in swing in *pendulum swing* in front support, back support and straddle support.

ii.   *False shear* (to the right)

From straddle support swing (right leg forward, left leg to the rear), swing to the right and elevate the right leg upwards and forwards in front of the horse. The left leg is then circled under the right leg, from the back to the front of the horse and both legs swing down in back support swing, legs apart. As the legs swing to the left, the *left leg is swung high in front of the horse* and then moves to the rear of the horse to commence the downswing in straddle support, pendulum swing. The false shear is now repeated as the legs swing once more to the right. Remember good weight transference is essential and up to three repetitions should be executed with good amplitude and rhythm.

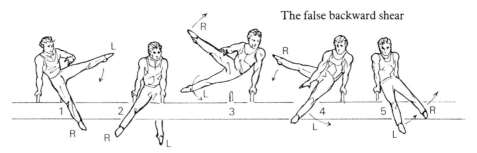

The false backward shear

iii. *Backward shear*

Perform, with good amplitude and rhythm, two good false backward shears as described in (ii) above and then continue the swing into a backward shear to the right with similar amplitude and rhythm.

iv. Repeat the above sequence for backward shear to the left.

v. Perform the following sequence: false shear backwards to the right; backward shear to right, false shear left; backward shear to left.

vi. Practise consecutive shears backwards to the right and to the left.

17.7 The double leg circle

A. The direction of rotation of the circle

It is necessary to clarify the method by which the direction of the circle is depicted in order that ambiguity can be eliminated. Consider the gymnast to be in *back support position* on the horse. If from this position he circles his legs to the left, then he would *circle left* or *anticlockwise* – and vice versa.

Throughout this text the descriptions will relate to a leftward double leg circle.

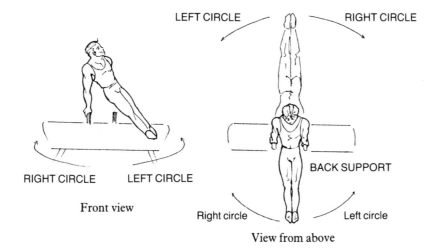

LEFT CIRCLE   RIGHT CIRCLE

BACK SUPPORT

RIGHT CIRCLE   LEFT CIRCLE

Front view

Right circle   Left circle

View from above

B.   The double leg circle technique

Circle left: side view

Circle left: front view

The following description of the main technical points of the circle should be read in conjunction with the diagrams above.

Note: the circle shown is a leftward (anticlockwise) circle.

 i. Throughout the circle the strong *shoulder lean should lead the body* and the shoulders should move away from the feet. Thus, the shoulders will describe an elliptical movement to counterbalance the legs.

 ii. As the *circle moves in a leftward direction the body will rotate about its vertical axis to the right.*

In one full circle left the body will rotate 360° about its long axis to the right.

iii.   In each quarter circle the body will rotate 90° to the right in order that the hips will always face the front of the horse. This is the minimum requirement and it is usual to rotate the body a little more than 90° in the quarter position (2 to 4) so that the hips face slightly to the right diagonal in position 4. This will ensure that the rotation of the body round the long axis will slightly precede the circle to ensure good technique in the circle and easy hand replacement.

iv.   The body should remain slightly dished to straight throughout the circle and there should always be clearance between the upper body, hips and arms.

The hip rotation

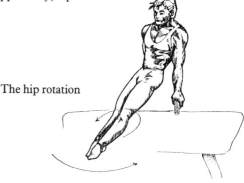

v.   The hands should be quickly returned to the handles upon regrasp so that the hands remain in contact with the handles for as long as possible. The hands and arms produce a torque action to draw the body through the circle.

C.   Developing the double leg circle

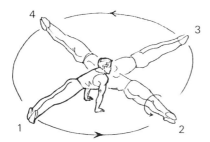

i.   Walk round the circle; emphasise the replacement of hands and the direction to which the hips face.

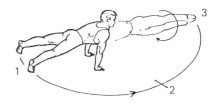

ii.   Swing through a half circle and then turn backwards to the right to front support. This encourages correct hip rotation.

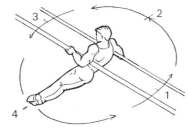

iii.   Double leg circle on parallel bars. Emphasis on amplitude in circle and correct hip turn.

iv.   Pommel machine (bucket). Many repetitions to improve awareness and support strength.

v. Mushroom trainer. Good shoulder
    displacement is necessary to elevate
    the body away from the mushroom.

vi. Floor level buck. Emphasise the
    continued shoulder movement and
    rhythm in the circle.

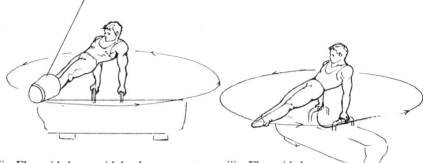

vii. Floor side horse with bucket support.

viii. Floor side horse.

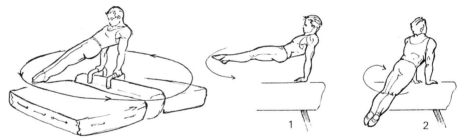

ix. Floor side horse with safety mat placed
    a) at the front then b) at the front and
    back of the horse – to create extension
    of the circle.

x. ½ circle (loop) facing along the horse
    with a ¼ turn inwards to stand facing
    the horse – encourages good hip
    rotation and rapid hand replacement.

xi. Loops facing along the horse without
    handles – hip amplitude at front of
    swing.

xii. Double leg circle on handles on full
     horse. Check direction hips face
     throughout the circle and clearance
     between the body and arms.

It should be noted that a great deal of time must be spent on ensuring a good technique in the circle before allowing the gymnast to progress to swinging on the full horse.

The following exercises will help to improve a) the amplitude in swing, b) the correct hip rotation, c) rapid replacement of the hands, d) a strong leg lift and shoulder lean as the body moves from back support to front support, e) good amplitude throughout the circle.

xiiia. Amplitude from front support to back support.

xiiib. Amplitude from back support to front support.

xiiic. Amplitude during both flank aspects in the circle.

xiva. Back support stretch.

xivb. Front support stretch.

xivc. Super lift of the body in front support.

The quality of circle developed by means of the exercises shown in (xiii) and (xiv) will ensure that the gymnast is able to attempt even the most difficult exercises with confidence and good technique.

D. Circling in various aspects of the horse

Once the circle has been mastered it should then be performed in all aspects of the horse without the 'shape' of the good quality double varying. It is only necessary to adjust the amount of shoulder displacement to accommodate the circle in the various positions on the horse.

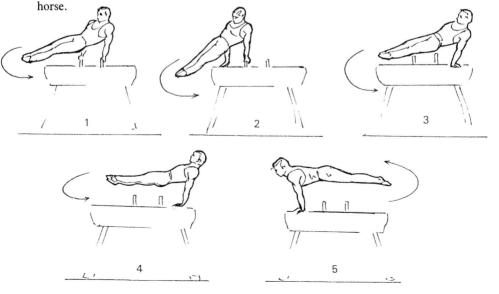

17.8   Downhill travel from circle

A.   The technique

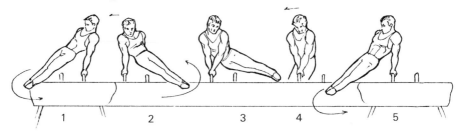

The circle should show good amplitude and correct hip alignment during phases 1 to 2 prior to commencing the travel from a back support position at 2. The right shoulder is moved to the right and during the period when the legs are swung from back support to front support the left hand is transferred in front of the body to be replaced on the left handle in front of the right hand (3). At position 4 the body weight should be balanced over the handle such that the centre line of the body is directly over the right handle. During the second half of the circle as the body moves to back support the right shoulder again leads the circle and the centre line of the body is moved between the right handle and the end of the horse; the right hand being replaced behind the body at 5, and the stretch in the circle is continued into the next circle by displacement of the weight from the left to the right hand.

Note: A similar technique, but stronger shoulder displacement, is used in the 'uphill' travel.

B.   Recommended progressive skills

i.   From back support position on the floor walk the body round in a double leg circle and transfer the hand positions to simulate the travel.

ii.   On the floor side horse the coach should support the gymnast at the legs and hips and 'shape' the gymnast through the travel. Emphasise amplitude in the circle, correct hip alignment and the balanced support over the one handle when in front support position.

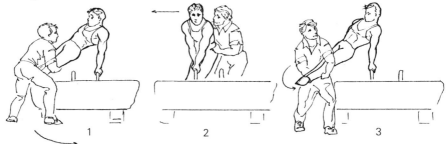

iii.   The gymnast would then perform a high number of repetitions of the skill in the bucket type training machine.

iv.   The next stage is to perform the travel unaided on the floor level side horse until it can be repeated a number of times without loss of form.

v. On the full horse, circle and travel out into *front* support and push off to land.

vi. The complete skill may then be attempted from a circle to travel into a circle on the full horse.

Remember, it is not necessary to change the shape of a well-groomed double leg circle. It is only necessary to transfer the shoulders and hands effectively to perform this travel efficiently.

17.9 The 'kreiskhre'

A. The technique

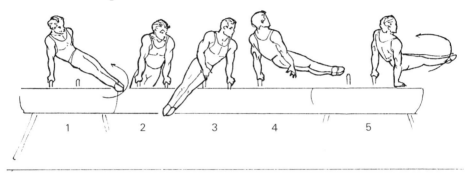

Upon replacement of the left hand in the front support position (2) the gymnast must thrust from the right hand to displace the left shoulder across the left handle (3). The right shoulder is then lifted to tilt the body and this will assist the body in making the ½ turn around the left arm (4). The body should remain extended as in a normal circle and the right hand should be replaced quickly behind the body on the end of the horse (5). There should always be clearance between the upper body, the hips and the supporting arm.

B. Progressive skills

i. On the floor make a half circle with 180° turn around the left arm from front support to finish in back support. Encourage the lifting of the right shoulder to tilt the body to the left.

ii. On a horse without the handles, coach to support and from the front support position tilt the shoulders and complete the kreiskhre (rear) to back support. Emphasise the shoulder tilt, extended body and rapid replacement of the right hand.

iii. Perform the kreiskhre on a floor horse with handles with the aid of a bucket trainer.

iv. The gymnast should then practise the element on the floor side horse without assistance until it is repeatedly performed with good technique.

v. The kreiskhre can now be attempted on the side horse and the coach should again encourage amplitude in the circle throughout the performance of the skill.

The kreiskhre can be performed in an uphill direction from the end on to the handles. It is commenced with the left hand on the left handle and the right hand on the end of the horse. A strong displacement of the left shoulder is essential to raise the centre of gravity of the body over the handle. Otherwise the technique is as described earlier for the kreiskhre (17.9A).

17.10 Combinations

When the double leg circle, the travel and the kreiskhre are competently performed as individual elements, they can be readily combined to form the *tramlot* (travel out kreiskhre in).

If the basic elements described in the earlier text on side horse are correctly taught they will form a good foundation for future more advanced work. Always encourage good technique and good form in all skills.

18.0 Rings

The main ingredients for good ring work are the ability to hold a stable handstand and the ability to perform a good basic swing towards a vertical line to the front and to the rear.

The handstand must be practised frequently on all apparatus and should be held for extended periods of time.

If the gymnast learns a good basic swing with correct technique from the outset this swing will be the foundation upon which the more advanced skills can be based.

18.1 Safety

The basic swing should be introduced with care, to reduce the risk of injury to the shoulders and lower back and to reduce the risk of falls.

During the performance of the swing the gymnast is most at risk as he passes through the vertical hang position on either the forward swing (heels leading) or backward swing (toes leading). The point just after the vertical position is the moment of greatest momentum and greatest force on the hands and it is the most likely point at which the gymnast may lose his grasp on the rings. It is essential that the coach develops the swing with good technique and offers support during the learning stages of the swing, until the gymnast is both adequately skilled and conditioned to perform the swing (see later for supporting arrangements).

Ensure that the gymnast effectively chalks the hands, and wears suitable handguards. Adequate landing surfaces and mats should be provided at all times.

18.2 The basic swing

A useful tip is to remember that on the rings the centre of gravity of the gymnast's body will move approximately up and down through the line of the ring frame uprights. The coach when supporting should therefore position himself in line with the vertical line of the ring frame, and when teaching the basic swing or introducing new elements a supporting platform or threequarter height ring (adjustable height rings) should be employed.

i.   The backward swing

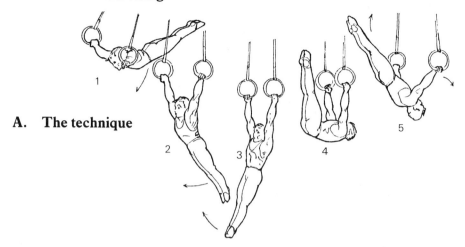

A.   The technique

During the downswing (1) the body should be straight at the hips (or slightly dished) with the rings pressed forward and above the shoulders to cause the chest to lead slightly in the downswing. The body should remain tensioned and the arms must be straight at all times.

As the body approaches the hang position (2) the hips are relaxed to lead the feet momentarily to permit a strong drive of the legs to occur through the bottom of the swing (3). During the hang phase the shoulder girdle should be strongly fixed to reduce 'bounce' and protect the shoulders against injury.

At the commencement of the upswing the feet should lead the swing and the body should form a deep dish at the hips. At 4 the shoulders are held down until the hips are above the shoulders and the legs are parallel with the arms. At this point, and not before, the rings may be turned so that the heel of the hand points rearwards (thumbs outwards). The rings are simultaneously passed backwards and open with straight arms to cause the body to rise (5). The feet should continue to lead the swing and the body should extend slightly into a dished shape – never permit a hollow in the body to occur.

During the downswing the shoulders lead the swing and the body should remain dished. The rings will be turned so that the heels of the hands point forwards and the arms are brought parallel behind the shoulders.

B.   Introducing the backward swing

i.   An awareness of the body shape and position of the rings can be established with the floor skills shown below.

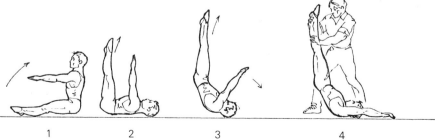

ii. On low rings the gymnast is raised into the correct shape with the shoulders held
down.

iii. On ¾ height rings the gymnast is encouraged to swing to the inverted position shown
above followed by a dished body swing down on straight arms. The coach must
support under the shoulders and at the underside of the thighs (rear of legs) during
both the upswing and the down swing.

iv. When the gymnast can competently swing into the position described in (iii) above the
gymnast may turn the rings and begin to move the rings rearwards and sideways. The
coach should ensure that the position described in (iii) above is achieved each time
before the rings are displaced and he should also assist under the thighs and shoulders
to produce elevation as the rings are moved.

v. Once fully aware of the technique the gymnast may now perform the swing on full
rings. The coach could support from a suitable platform as shown.

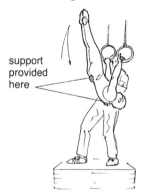

support
provided
here

ii. The forward swing

A. The technique

During the downward swing the body is held in a dished shape, the rings are taken
backwards behind the shoulders and the rings are turned so that the heel of the hand faces
towards the feet. The upper back and shoulders should lead the swing and the arms must be
straight at all times during the downswing phase (4 to 6).

As the body approaches the vertical hang position the heels are accelerated backwards to
lead the body (7). Again the shoulder girdle should be tensioned throughout the hang
position. As the body approaches the vertical hang *the hands should be rotated so that the heel
of the hand faces out over.* This will facilitate a degree of rotation in the shoulder joint during
the upswing.

The rings are moved slightly to the side to permit rotation in the shoulder joint, *but the shoulders are held down*. The heels continue to drive upwards to lead the swing until the hips are above the level of the shoulders (8 to 9). At this point the rings are taken backwards in line with the hips and the gymnast presses down strongly on the rings. The press on the rings is accompanied by the sucking in of the chest to produce a dished body shape. This provides a good tensioned body against which the pressing force on the rings can react to elevate the body above the rings (10). The head should be held in a neutral position during this pressing phase.

Before commencing the downswing the gymnast must quickly press the rings forwards and parallel to permit the chest to lead the body slightly during the downswing.

B.   Introducing the forward swing

i.   An understanding of the basic technique should first be introduced on the floor as shown below.

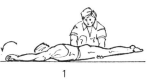

In position 1 the hands have been rotated outwards to simulate the hang position below the rings. The heels are raised to lead the body and the rings move to the side – shoulders are held down (2). As the legs and hips continue to rise the hands are taken behind the shoulders (3). When the hips are raised above the shoulders the gymnast presses strongly downwards and the chest is drawn in to cause the body to rise and the upper back begins to lead the swing (4).

ii.   On low rings the coach supports under the thighs and under the deltoid (shoulders) to create the correct pattern of movement.

iii.   Using ¾ height rings such that the gymnast can just clear the landing surface in vertical hang and with the coach on a suitable platform, the coach supports as described in (ii) above – the gymnast performs the swing initially only as far as the position shown in position 2 above. As the gymnast's awareness improves he may progress to 3 and 4 with the coach providing good support.

iv.   Once the gymnast can competently perform the swing on ¾ rings he may progress to full height rings, but the coach, standing on a suitable platform, should offer assistance in the initial stages.

iii.   The complete swing

When the gymnast fully understands each aspect of the forward and backward swing he may combine the two swings together. The aim should be to swing towards a vertical line at both the front and rear of the swing.

If this technique is adopted then the gymnast will be equipped to progress towards the more advanced elements without having to 'doctor' the swing. With improved strength and awareness the gymnast should readily relate this swing to even the most advanced skills.

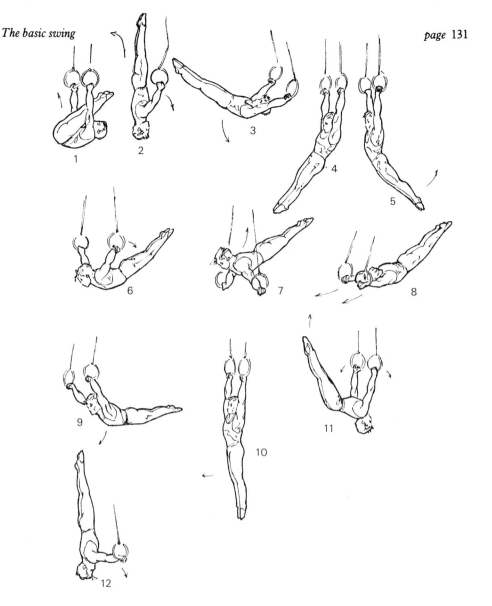

18.3   The static dislocation

A.   The technique

From the inverted hang position the body should fold into a deep pike with the hips remaining in front of the rings (1). The body should then be struck out to the rear to an angle of about 30° above the rings. As the strike commences the hands should be turned so that the heels of the hands face towards the feet to enable force to be applied quickly to the rings (2). The rings are pressed out to the side with a downward force causing the body to rise above the rings (3). The rings should then be forced quickly in front of the shoulders and the body should be tensioned in a straight position prior to commencing the downswing (4). The rings should move above the shoulder line to cause the chest to lead in the downswing but the hips should *not* be allowed to relax.

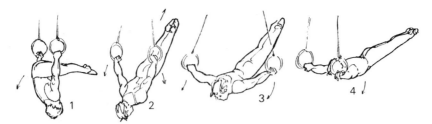

B.   Introducing the static dislocation

i.   Commence the teaching either on the floor or on low rings. The coach must support under the chest and under the thighs to assist in the elevation and ensure good direction of the leg strike.

ii.   Perform the dislocation from static on ¾ height rings with the coach supporting as shown above, but the coach must now allow the gymnast to swing controlled through to hang position. Emphasise the need to lead the downswing with the chest, body straight and arms straight.

iii.   Once the gymnast is confident he may progress to full height rings, with initial attempts being supported by the coach from a platform.

18.4   The straight body or giant dislocation

A.   The technique

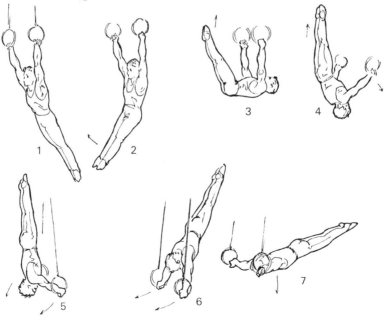
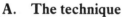

It should be noted that the swing shown in positions 1 to 4 is identical to that described for the basic backward swing (18.2i). From 4 the feet continue to lead the swing and the body is held in a slightly dished shape. The rings are first turned so the heel of the hand faces away from the body. The rings are then pressed backwards, outwards and then downwards to elevate the body (5). The rings continue to press forwards under the shoulders and should be brought to a position in front of the body, arms parallel prior to the downswing commencing (6). The body should remain straight and the chest will lead the downswing. The angle in the shoulders should be totally removed prior to the body passing the horizontal position with the rings (7). The chest continues to lead the downswing until a hang position is reached at which point the legs are accelerated to commence the upswing.

B.   Introducing the straight body dislocation

i.   Before commencing the dislocation it is essential that the gymnast is fully conversant with the skill required in the descent phase (bail down part). This bail down part should be taught first on low rings.

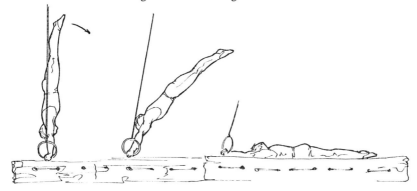

ii.   The bail down should now be taught on ¾ rings with the coach supporting under the chest and thighs to absorb the downswing and maintain a straight body in the gymnast. Once this has been effectively mastered the bail can be performed on high rings with the coach standing on a suitable platform and supporting the gymnast under the chest and thighs in the downswing. *Note:* the danger point for the gymnast is at its greatest when he swings through the hang position and the coach should be well prepared to support the gymnast at this point, until the swing down (bail) has been successfully learnt.

iii.   Since the understanding of the upward swing will have been taught previously the gymnast may now rehearse the swing over the rings in a ground simulation situation.

1	2	3	4	5

iv. This aspect of the skill can now be developed on low rings with two supports, one taking the shoulders as shown, the other taking the chest and thighs for the downswing.

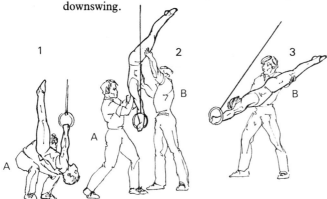

v. On ¾ rings and with the coach standing on a platform, the gymnast swings towards the inverted position and the coach reaches through the rings to take the legs with the second hand and places the first hand under the shoulder. The coach now elevates and shapes the gymnast through the dislocation and controls the gymnast throughout the downswing.

Care must be taken to avoid inhibiting the 'circling' action of the rings.

vi. The gymnast may now progress to full height rings. The coach standing on a platform assists the gymnast in the upswing under the thighs and chest and then quickly transfers the hands to support the gymnast under the chest and under the thighs for the downswing. *Note:* the gymnast must not lose the tight, straight body shape when the force is applied to the rings to elevate the shoulders.

Having circled over the rings and moved the rings forwards the gymnast may initially release the rings at position 3 to land on the feet. Once the gymnast repeatedly produces the correct form and technique up to position 3 he may then retain the grasp on the rings and continue the downswing with the coach controlling the swing.

C. Useful strengthening exercises

    i.   Using elasticated strands

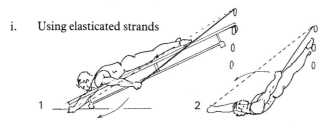

    ii.   On the floor

    iii.   Ring trolley trainer

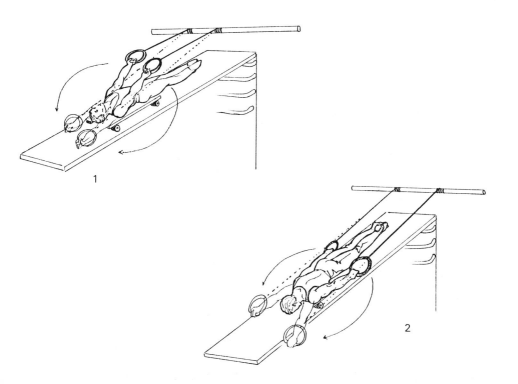

18.5   The straight body back salto dismount

A.   The technique

The swing from position 1 to 3 is as described for the basic swing but at 3 the body is extended to increase inertia and reduce the rotation of the body. This extension of the body is accompanied by the rings being pressed quickly backwards and sideways to cause elevation of the body. At 4, with the body straight to slightly arched, and in front of the vertical line through the ring uprights, the rings are released to the side. The body will now rotate about its centre of gravity during the flight. The shoulders are lifted backwards and the arms are moved sideways to reduce inertia and increase rotation (5). Prior to landing the arms are raised above the shoulders to increase the length of the body and reduce rotation for landing purposes.

Note:

1.   The body should *not* pass through the rings before the release.
2.   Piking down from 5 into landing should be discouraged and rotation created by raising the chest and shoulders.

B.   Introducing the straight back salto dismount

i.   The prerequisite must be a good upward swing as shown in positions 1 to 3.

ii.   The following skill can be used to develop an awareness of the salto. It is performed from a static supported hang on ¾ height rings. Position 1 should simulate the body shape and point of release of the rings. In 2, with the coaches supporting under the thighs and under the deltoid/biceps area of the arms, cause the shoulders to be elevated backwards to simulate the rotation and elevation of the salto. Landing should be in a demi plié position.

iii. Again on ¾ height rings and with the coaches supporting as shown in the diagrams above, the gymnast performs the back salto from a good swing.

iv. Once the skill is effectively mastered it can now be performed on high rings with the coach operating from platforms and handling the gymnast with the same supporting arrangements.

v. When the gymnast is competent in performing the skill he may be encouraged to gain additional elevation by preceding the salto by a swinging straight body dislocation. The coach must support initially under the thighs and upper back on the upswing until release of the rings and then transfer to the chest and back to control the landing.

Note: The straight back salto shown is suitable for the later introduction of twists into the salto.

18.6 The straight body inlocation

A. The technique

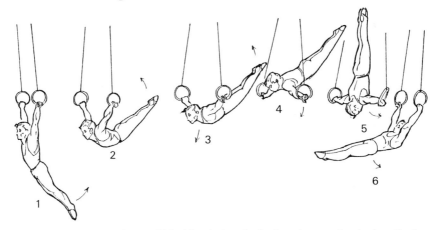

The swing up to position 4 will be identical to the basic swing previously described.

It should be remembered that the shoulders are held down at 2 and 3 until the hips are above the level of the shoulders. At position 4 the rings are taken sideways and rearwards under the body while the arms press down on the rings to elevate the body. The body shape should be altered from an arched to straight shape, a good postural shape to maximise the effect of the downward press on the rings.

The rings continue to be pressed to the rear, and move to a parallel arm position just prior to the downswing commencing. During the downswing a small angle should be introduced between the arms and the body, the body should be slightly dished and the shoulders/upper back should lead the downswing. The head should be neutral throughout the skill.

B. Introducing the straight body inlocation

i. The prerequisite must be the ability to produce a good forward swing to a position as illustrated in position 3 in the diagrams showing the inlocation technique.

ii. The inlocation can be simulated on the floor as shown below.

5   4   3   2   1

iii.   The skills should now be 'shaped' on low rings from a static hang.

4   3   2   1

iv.   The gymnast may now perform the straight body inlocation on ¾ height rings with the coach supporting from a platform. The gymnast must produce a good and powerful swing, the coach supports under the chest and thighs on the upswing and then transfers quickly to support at the thighs and back of the chest at the start of the downswing after the inlocation.

Note: 1. When teaching this skill to young boys it may help to encourage the head to be lifted backwards, to delay the shoulder drop, until the shoulders are above the rings. Later the head will be held in a neutral position.

2. During the pressing phase with the hips above the shoulders, emphasise the production of the straight body shape with the chest sucked in.

v.   The gymnast may now perform the skill on full height rings with the coach supporting from a suitable platform and assisting as described in (iv) above.

C.   Useful strengthening exercises

i.   Elasticated strands

ii.   On floor

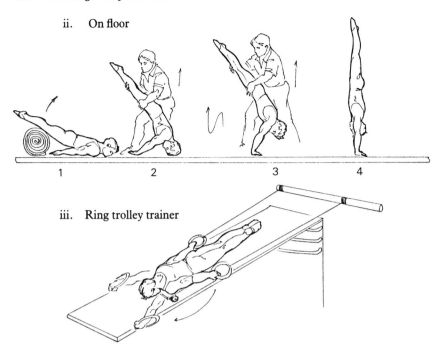

iii.   Ring trolley trainer

18.7   Stemme backwards to support (back uprise)

A.   The technique

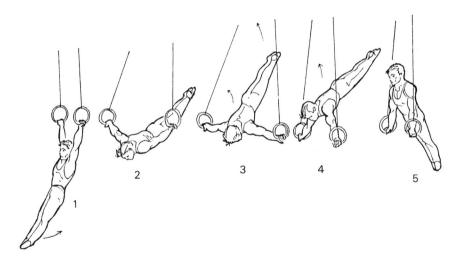

Again, this skill is developed from a good basic swing with the shoulders held down until the hips are above the shoulders. The hands at 3 are taken backwards under the body and to the side. The rings are then pressed downwards to come together, shoulder width apart, under the body, while the tensioned body continues to rise. The shoulders are taken in front of the rings to assist in the control of the downward swing into support.

B. Introducing the backwards stemme

i. A prerequisite is to swing to the inverted position shown at position 2 above with the hips above the level of the shoulders.

ii. The gymnast may be lifted through the skill on the floor with emphasis on the body shape and action of the rings closing under the body.

iii. Using a similar support to that shown above in (ii) the gymnast should be supported through the skill from:

a. Static hang on low rings.
b. Swing in hang on ¾ height rings.
c. Swing in hang on full height rings.

Note: A common error in performing the back stemme is to press on the rings too early before the hips are above the shoulders, causing the shoulders to rise early resulting in the feet dropping. Always ensure that the head is neutral and that the hips are above the shoulders prior to the action of pressing down on the rings.

If this skill is taught correctly it may eventually be performed into handstand without affecting the basic technique.

18.8 The straight body front salto dismount

A. The technique

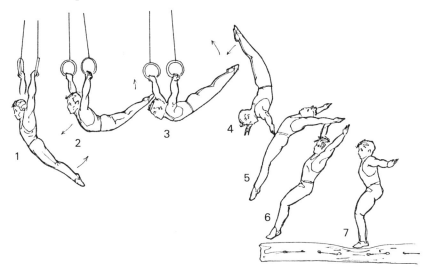

The swing follows a similar pattern to the basic advocated swing up to position 3. At this point the rings are opened and the hands released with strong heel drive having raised the hips above the shoulders. Upon release the drive of the legs is maintained by arching the heels over the head (4). The arch is retained through 5 but the body is then quickly dished to anticipate the landing which should be in a demi plié position.

B.   Introducing the straight front salto dismount

i.   A good basic swing is an essential prerequisite.

ii.   The skill can then be shaped on low rings with the coaches supporting under the shoulders across the deltoid/biceps and under the thighs on the upswing. Upon release the hand on the thighs should be quickly transferred to the lower back to support the landing.

iii.   Once the spatial awareness and understanding of the skill has been established the skill may be performed from swings, firstly on ¾ height rings then on high rings. The coach/coaches support in a similar way to that described in (ii) above.

Note: Care should be taken to restrict over-rotation upon landing by maintaining contact with the gymnast's shoulders throughout the skill.

C.   The piked front salto dismount

The piked front salto dismount can be developed in a similar manner to that described for the straight body salto. The difference occurs upon release of the rings. With the hips above the shoulders upon release the legs are stopped and the momentum transferred from the legs to the chest to allow the chest to fold deeply into a pike against the legs. The chest is then stopped and the momentum is transferred back to the legs, which then kick to extend the body towards the landing.

18.9   The upstart or kip

A.   The technique

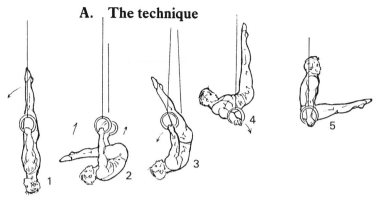

The upstart commences from inverted hang with a deep pike in which the hips are held just slightly above the shoulder level. The reaction gained from the rapid folding of the body is utilised in striking the hips and legs upwards along the vertical line through the rings. As the body moves upwards the gymnast pulls downwards and outwards on the rings to cause the shoulders to rise (3). The rings are rapidly turned so that the heel of the hand faces outwards, the position of the feet is fixed, and the rings are forced forwards, outwards and downwards to cause the upper body to rise through the rings and towards the legs (4). The rings are pressed downwards to the side of the body and the body is lowered from a dish to a piked half lever support position at 5.

B.   Introducing the upstart

   i.   The exercise shown above utilises an elasticated band and is usefully employed in developing the sequence of actions and understanding of shape necessary in the execution of the upstart.

   ii.   The gymnast should then be supported on the low rings with the coach assisting with one hand on the hamstrings, the other on the gymnast's lower back.

   iii.   Once the gymnast is strong enough and has a good understanding of the technique he may progress to high rings.

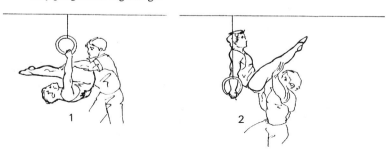

C.   Useful strengthening exercises for the upstart

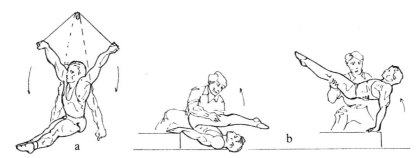

18.10   Bent body press to handstand

A.   The technique

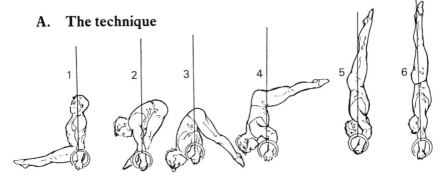

When pressing to handstand it is essential that the centre of gravity remains over the support point (the hands) throughout the element. From the half lever position the shoulders are drawn forward of the hands as the seat is elevated above the shoulders (2).

When the seat is above the shoulders the arms bend to ease the lift of the seat into the vertical position over the hands (3). From this position of balance the position of the hips is fixed over the hands and the legs begin to lift (4). The press with the arms commences assisted by the action of the legs towards a vertical position (5).

The handstand is completed by the straightening of the arms extending the body into a straight position, and the hands turning outwards slightly (6).

Note: To remain 'on balance' the hands (rings) must be held directly under the centre of gravity of the body.

B.   Introducing the bent body press to handstand

   i.   On floor perform bent body headstand into press to handstand (fig. i).

ii.   On low parallel bars practise ½ lever, lift until seat is above the shoulders then dip the
      shoulders by bending the arms but continue to lift the seat into a bent arm piked
      handstand balance. Then combine the arm press with the extension of the hips to raise
      the legs into handstand. Ensure that the gymnast does not lose the dished body shape
      during the press (fig. ii).

iii. The gymnast should now perform a bent body press to handstand from a platform
      which provides a starting position with the seat already above the shoulders (fig. iii).

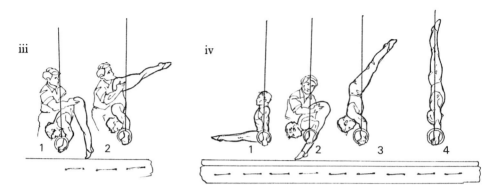

iv.   The bent arm press to handstand can now be practised from the half lever position on
      the low rings. The coach should support the gymnast at the hips to assist the press and
      to maintain the centre of gravity over the hands (fig. iv).

v.   Once the condition of the gymnast improves he may attempt the lift to handstand on
      low rings with the coach holding the rings still to create a more stable base.

vi.   When the gymnast achieves the handstand position he must be encouraged to practise
      holding the handstand position for progressively increasing periods of time. This is
      best achieved by maintaining a straight (not arched) body shape, and with straight
      arms, adjusting the ring position to keep the rings beneath the centre of gravity.

      Note: The wrists should be locked straight and not flexed and the hands should be
      slightly turned outwards to clear the arms from the rings.

C.   Conditioning for the press to handstand

i.   The handstand is an important skill in gymnastics and frequent practice of this skill on
      various apparatus is essential to develop good strength and control in the handstand
      position.

ii.   Regular practice of a high number of repetitions of those exercises shown above as
      developmental skills will also develop the condition.

iii. Further exercises can be seen in section 12.6g above.

19.0 Vaulting

Vaults are generally categorised as being either:

    i. *Singular rotational:* such as the handspring vault in which the rotation onto the horse and off the horse is in the same direction.

    or

    ii. *Counter-rotational:* in which the direction of the flight off the horse is opposed to the rotation of the flight onto the horse, i.e. squat and straddle vaults.

19.1 The aspects of vaulting

When describing vaulting techniques it is helpful to consider the following aspects within each vault.

A. The run-up

The main purpose of the run-up is to develop controlled horizontal velocity and momentum through a gradual acceleration over a consistent and measured approach.

During the run-up the eyes should be focused on the horse and springboard to gauge the point of take-off. Good running style should be developed with knee lift, rhythmic arm action, body tilting slightly forward and good balanced stride length. Sprint training over 20 metres, resistance running (weighted or against a partner's resistance), uphill running, will help to develop strength in running.

B. The pre-jump

The pre-jump is the phase which translates the run-up into a contact on the springboard with high horizontal momentum. During the last few strides of the run, and quite often in the last stride, the arms are taken behind the body to assist in the forward drive onto the board. In the hurdle step (the push from the front foot to land on the board with two feet together) the arms are driven forward and the feet are moved forward to lead the hips onto the board.

The flight-on to the board should have a low trajectory with the distance from point of take-off to board contact being around 1½ times the body length for best results.

The pre-jump should be taught as a skill in its own right until it can be effectively performed consistently, prior to combining it with a vault.

Introduce the pre-jump as a floor skill – hitting a target area and then onto a board with a take-off onto a safety mattress landing.

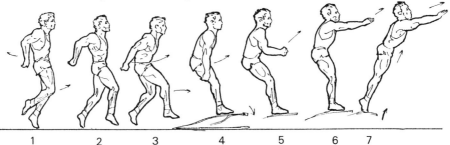

    1   2   3   4   5   6   7

C.   The take-off

During the contact with the board, the board is first compressed by the forward momentum and trajectory of the pre-jump, then the arms are driven forward and the body will rotate about the feet. The forward lean of the body, the drive of the arms in a forward and upward direction and the return force from the board will combine in developing the flight and forward rotation at take-off.

The gymnast should be encouraged to reduce the time interval for contact on the board to a minimum (around 0.15 secs is normal) to maintain the forward momentum (see the illustration in (B) above.

D.   The pre-flight

This is the phase which comprises the release from the board and the initial flight onto the horse. The distance from the take-off point on the board to the contact point on the horse should be around 1½ times the body length for best results. It should be noted that once the feet leave the board the body will rotate around the centre of gravity of the body but also that the degree of rotation required for different categories of vault will vary. Refer to individual vault descriptions for more detail, but generally overswing vaults (handsprings, etc.) require greater rotation than counter-rotational vaults such as squats or straddle vaults. The shape of the body and angle of contact with the horse will also vary according to the type of vault to be performed.

i.   Flight for squat vault   ii.   Flight for handspring vault

E.   The thrust and horse contact

In order that the momentum of the body is not lost, particularly in a handspring vault, the repulsion or thrust from the horse must be rapid. This requires good body tension and strong upper body, shoulders and arms to create the powerful thrust either to add to height and rotation in the case of the handspring or to produce counter-rotation in the case of the squat or straddle vaults. Refer to individual vaults for more detail. An early thrust requires friction between the hands and the horse – always ensure that the surface of the horse will provide good frictional contact.

F.   The post-flight

The path of the centre of gravity during the post-flight will have been established during the thrusting phase from the horse; the height, distance and flight time will vary according to the type of vault being performed. The post-flight usually contains the essence of the vault in which the shape of the body and spatial awareness are predominant features. The degree of rotation can be affected during flight insofar as a reduction in body length (tucking, piking, hollowing) will *increase* rotation while a long body will rotate more slowly.

G.   The landing

During the landing the gymnast must gradually reduce the forward momentum and the rotation of the body to bring the body to rest in a safe and controlled standing position.

It is essential that the feet contact the landing surface in front of the body and the legs gradually absorb the momentum of the body by producing a controlled demi plié position while the upper body is retarded through a raising of the arms, upwards and to the side, in order to produce a stable position.

The landing must be frequently practised as a skill in is own right with the controlled demi plié with flat back being emphasised at all times. Practise the landing from a platform, jumping upwards, forwards, backwards and with the inclusion of twist.

The landing surface should constitute a module which will absorb shock and impact but must not be too soft as this could cause instability and possible twisting injuries to the ankles and knees. A competition landing module, usually carpet covered, or a safety mat covered with an agility mattress, is recommended.

19.2   The bent leg squat vault on long horse

A.   The technique

The flight from the board should be low with the arms reaching forward to contact the horse with the body just above horizontal and a slight angle between the arms and body (4).

A strong shoulder and arm thrust against the horse must occur, with the hands ahead of the shoulders, to produce the necessary lift and counter-rotation from the hands. The shoulders will rise and the tuck is created by closing the angle in the hips and bending the leg at the knees. The arms should lift backwards, sideways and upwards during the post-flight phase (5).

Prior to landing, the chest is held upright and the feet are kicked forward to anticipate the landing (6). Upon contact with the landing surface the gymnast should land with a demi plié action, the arms moving downwards to the side to maintain the balance.

B.   Introducing the squat vault on long horse

i.   Before the vault is introduced on a long horse the gymnast must be able to perform the squat vault on a cross horse with good flight and control.

ii.   On the long horse, perform the layout flight-on, to squat on the horse, and extended body jump-off to land.

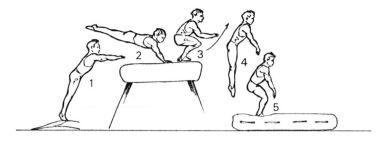

iii.   Squat vault from a platform.

Note: Ensure that the head is held up at all times. There is a tendency for gymnasts to drop the head, causing poor flight and lack of shoulder lift.

iv.   One of the most difficult aspects for a young gymnast to comprehend is the strong thrust and lift of the shoulders from the horse. The following exercises will help an understanding of the skill and will also improve the thrusting condition.

v.   The gymnast may now attempt the squat vault over the long horse from a spring board take-off with the emphasis on the push from the hands and elevation of the shoulders. The coach should stand at the side of the horse and assist the gymnast under the chest and across the back as shown. The coach must make early contact with the gymnast's chest and must travel with the gymnast during the flight-off.

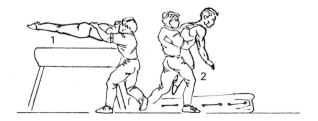

vi.   Once the gymnast can perform the vault competently with the above support, the
gymnast may now perform the vault unaided but the coach will stand at the front of the
horse to support at the upper arm during the flight-off.

19.3   The straight leg squat on long horse

A.   The technique

The gymnast must have a forward lean at take-off and the flight-on is low, arriving at contact
with the horse with the arms reaching ahead of the shoulders and the hips horizontal to the
shoulders. The strong thrust from the arms and shoulders must occur with the shoulders
behind the hands to enable a powerful uplift of the shoulders to occur (4). As the reaction to
the thrust occurs from the horse the hips are rapidly elevated, the feet are snapped forward
to pike the body and the arms begin to move backwards (5). The arms continue to circle
backwards, sideways and upwards while the body, once the feet are clear of the horse,
begins to extend (6). The predominant action here should be to elevate the chest to extend
the body (7). In anticipation of the landing the feet should be kicked forward to contact the
landing surface ahead of the body (8).

B.   Developing the straight leg squat vault

i.   The prerequisite is the ability competently to perform a bent leg squat vault over the
long horse, as described in section 19.2.

ii.   Rehearsal of the following body action will be valuable in understanding the body
action in the vault: jump, dish, hollow, dish, with good body tension.

iii.   The vault should first be performed over a cross horse with the coaches supporting
from the front of the horse and rear of the horse as shown.

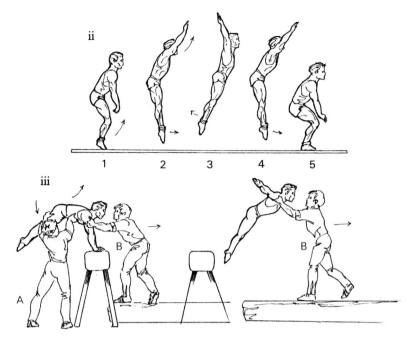

Coach A feeds the legs into the pike and then assists the chest to lift in the flight from the horse. Coach B supports at the rear of the horse holding the gymnast's upper arms and stepping backwards to assist the flight-off.

iv.   The vault may now be performed in the situation shown below, with the emphasis being placed upon the strong thrust and elevation of the shoulders together with the correct body action.

The coach may assist from the side of the horse under the chest and behind the legs as shown by coach A in (iii) above.

v.   The vault is now performed on the long horse with coaches initially supporting from the side of the horse and at the rear of the horse as shown in (iii) above.

19.4   The straddle vault on long horse

A.   The technique

The flight onto the horse, contact and thrust from the horse is identical to that of the squat vaults. However, at position 4, as the thrust occurs, the feet snap down wider into a straddle position to create a *slight dish* in the body. The drive of the feet is then arrested and the chest

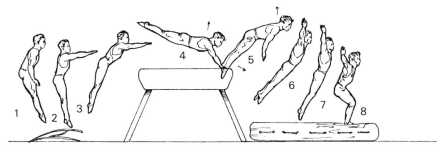

and arms elevated to straighten the body (5). The legs are then closed as they snap forward again to anticipate the landing (7 and 8).

B.   Developing the straddle vault over long horse

   i.   The straddle vault on cross horse must be competently performed prior to developing the vault on long horse.

  ii.   The vault is first performed from a platform situation over a lengthways buck.

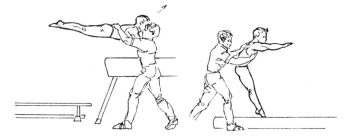

            The coach supports on the chest and back to elevate the upper body but the coach must move rapidly forward with the gymnast to avoid inhibiting the legs during the straddle.

 iii.   The coach may similarly handle the gymnast through the vault with a springboard take-off.

 iv.   Progress should then be made to perform the vault over a long horse with the coach supporting as illustrated in (ii) above.

  v.   As the gymnast gains in confidence and masters the vault he may then attempt the vault unaided, but the coach should stand at the landing side of the horse, facing the gymnast, in readiness to support the gymnast at the upper arms or around the chest in the advent of an unsuccessful attempt.

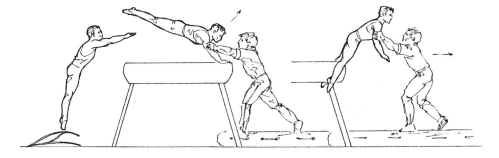

19.5   The handspring vault

A.   The technique

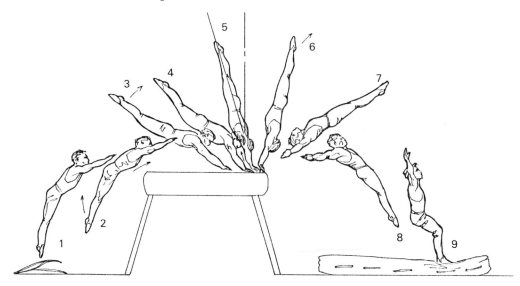

The gymnast must leave the board slightly leaning forward and with high forward momentum (1). The legs should be driven strongly from the board to cause forward rotation while the arms reach along the horse (2 and 3). It should be noted that the leg drive creates the hollow shape during flight and *not* a relaxation of the hips or dropping of the chest. The chest is held 'open' and the hamstring muscles and gluteal muscles used to drive the legs above the line of the shoulder (3). The flight onto the horse must be fairly low but with good forward rotation and the hands should contact the horse with the chest low and the legs at around 30° to the horizontal through the shoulders. A small angle should also be set between the body and arms (4).

The thrust through the arms should commence immediately the hands contact the horse and, due to the rotation of the body, the reaction from the horse should cause the hands to leave the horse at around 8° before the vertical position (5). To gain maximum effect from the thrust phase the head should be held slightly backwards to neutral, the body should be extended upwards to a straight position with the chest in, and a strong push from the arms and shoulders will produce good elevation and sufficient rotation. From the release point the arms are taken backwards, sideways and downwards to reduce the length of the body (reduces inertia) to increase rotation (6). The head is taken forward to maintain the straight body shape and to allow early spotting of the landing surface (7). The hips are then relaxed and the heels forced downwards to anticipate the landing (8). The arms may be raised again to reduce the rotation for landing (9). The landing should be in a demi plié position.

Note: There are a variety of similar techniques used in the performance of the handspring vault but the above description is a proven technique which will lend itself readily to developing into a handspring with twist.

B. Developing the handspring vault

i.   An understanding of the handspring skill on floor may be a useful prerequisite to the handspring vault.

ii. The necessary powerful leg drive can be developed by regular use of the conditioning exercise below which will strengthen the hamstring, gluteal and low back muscles.

iii.

iv.

v.

vi. The flight-off

The coach must take care to control over-rotation upon landing.

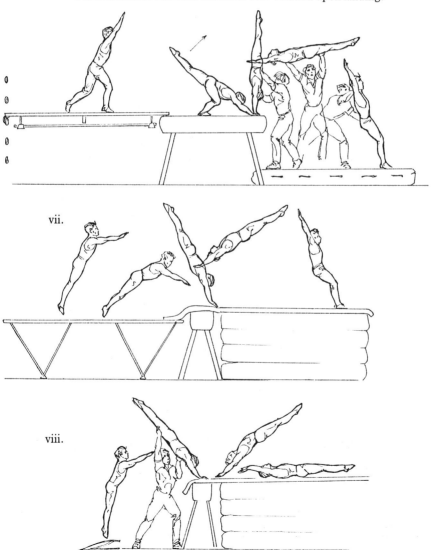

vii.

viii.

ix.

x.

xi.

xii.

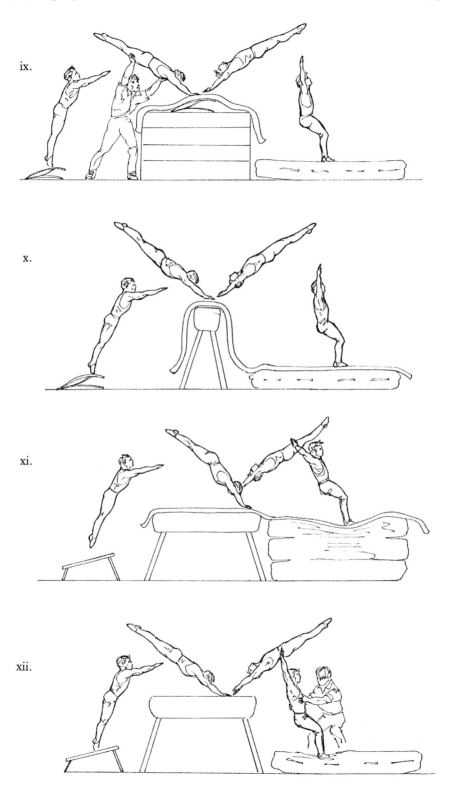

xiii.

Note:

1. The use of a trampoline or trampette situation as shown in (v) permits a large number of repetitions without the dangers of over-use injury and fatigue.
2. The use of padded apparatus as illustrated in figs. v to viii reduces the impact upon the wrists and body and will therefore permit more repetitions to be safely performed.
3. The coach should always ensure that the correct flight-on with sufficient rotation is emphasised.
4. The coach must always be aware of the possibility of over-rotation during the post-flight phase and must be prepared to support at the chest or arms to ensure a safe landing during the learning stages.

20.0 Parallel bars

To enable a gymnast to become proficient on parallel bars it is essential for him to develop a complete command of the basic forms of swing in each of the following positions.

Swing in support on the hands, and underside of the upper arms; swing in piked hang, dished hang and full hang position under the bar.

To achieve these swings the gymnast must possess good upper body support strength and good postural control of the body.

20.1 Swing in full support to handstand

A. The technique

In the handstand position (1), the gymnast should hold a fully extended handstand with straight body. The downswing is then initiated by extending out of the shoulders and dishing the body to move the feet out of balance (2). Once the downswing has commenced the shoulders begin to move forwards slightly in front of the hands to maintain a degree of control on the swing (3). The downswing may be performed with a straight body until position 4 where the hips relax to lead the feet, *or* the hips may relax at a horizontal position with the shoulders.

Either technique is acceptable and is selected to suit the preference of the gymnast. From this hip leading position at position 4, the legs are strongly accelerated through the support position at position 5, to lead with the feet on the upswing, and the shoulders are taken slightly backwards behind the hands at position 6. The legs continue to drive upwards,

creating a dished body swing to shorten the length of the body for the upswing (7). When the centre of gravity and the hips are above the line of the shoulders the gymnast presses down against the bars to force the shoulders forward of the hands and extend the body (8) in readiness for the downswing to give maximum potential swing.

The straight to dished body shape is held throughout the downswing and the shoulders move slightly behind the hands offering some control on the swing. At position 10 the hips are drawn in to create a deeper dish in the body in order to create an action from which the heels can be accelerated through the support position (11) to begin to lead the swing with a very slightly arched body on the upswing (12). The shoulders must now lean forwards to bring the centre of gravity towards the hands to reduce the length of lever (and reduce inertia) on the upswing (13). As the body passes through the horizontal position the chest is 'drawn in' and the upper back begins to lead the body towards handstand (14). As the gymnast approaches the handstand the shoulders are brought backwards over the hands to lengthen the body and thus decelerate the body into a controlled handstand position (15). On arrival in handstand the body should be tensioned in a straight shape and the shoulders should be fully extended.

Notes:

1. During the swing through support at positions 5 and 11 the gymnast must rotate the elbows backwards and inwards to 'lock' the arms to prevent collapse and he must also press down the arms strongly to maintain a good support position.

2. It is during the support phase that the gymnast is most likely to fail and the coach must be continually aware of this possibility and offer good support during the initial learning stage – see p. 159.

3. It is recommended that during the initial learning stages young boys who lack good support strength are not encouraged to move the shoulders forward at position 8 or this will produce, for them, an excessive downswing. The shoulder movement forward of the hand is introduced at a later stage when the gymnast is strong and has a better understanding of the swing.

4. The head should be positioned as shown in the diagrams above.

5. Do not permit the gymnast to hollow the back (relaxed abdominals) during the swing towards handstand as this will be detrimental to performance.

B. Developing the swing in support

i. Shaping and positioning the gymnast.

ii. Introducing the swing.

iii. Stopping the swing – by straddling the legs across padded bars.

a. Front swing

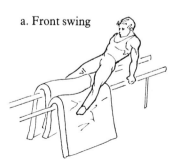

b. Back swing

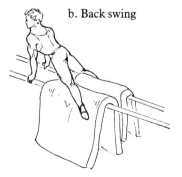

iv. Frequent practice of kicking and pressing into handstand and holding handstand on mini parallel bars.

v. Swing and dismount forwards.

vi. Swing and dismount backwards.

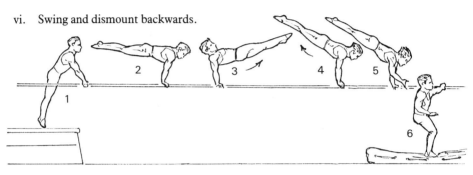

vii. Full swing.

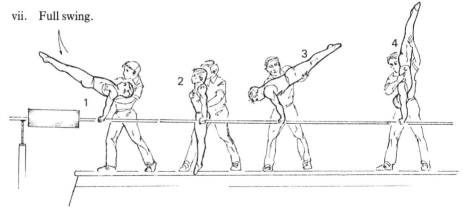

20.2 Forward uprise from upper arm support

A. The technique

The gymnast must at all times press down on the bars to maintain a high support position to enable a good swing to be established. During the initial downswing (1), the body is extended and straight, then as the body passes below the bars the hips relax to produce a hip leading action (2 and 3) from which the legs may be driven forwards and upwards into a 'dished' shape to commence the upswing (4 and 5). When the hips are in line with the bars the feet are decelerated and the hips extended to reduce the rotation of the body (6). This is accompanied by a strong press down on the bars to cause the body to rise above the bars (7). The press must continue throughout the upswing to produce an extended body position with the shoulders in support over the hands in readiness for the downswing (8).

A second technique may also be used in which at position 6 the legs continue to drive into a vertical line and the seat is pressed upwards towards a Russian Vee support position as shown below.

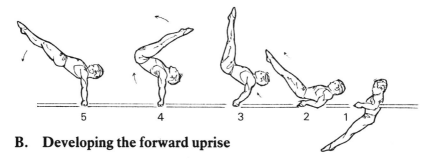

B.   Developing the forward uprise

i.   The swing: swinging in upper arm hang and driving to a straight body position; maintain a high support at all times.

ii.   Conditioning and understanding of the arm press: repeat many times.

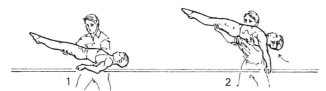

iii.   Uprise to straddle the bar: support from beneath and between the bars.

iv.   With the coach supporting from beneath and between the bars as shown in (iii) above, the gymnast performs the complete uprise with the legs together but *the coach must remain in support to control the downswing after completion of the uprise.*

Note: The straddling of the bars is also a useful safety precaution to be used by the gymnast in an abortive attempt.

20.3 Backward roll

A. The technique

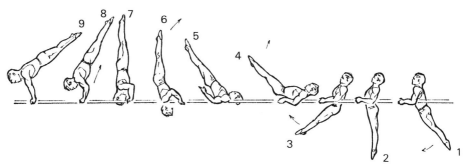

From the hollow back position at 1 the legs are accelerated to lead the upswing (2 and 3) with the body shape changing to a 'deep dish'. When the hips move above the line of the bar (4) the body begins to extend to reduce rotation and the gymnast presses the elbows downwards to cause the upper body to rise above the bars. With a final rapid press against the bars, the arms are rotated backwards (5). At this point it is possible to develop a little flight from the bars to elevate the body, allow greater time for replacement of the hands, and improve the technique for the pressing phase (6). The gymnast must reach backwards for the bars to regrasp with the angle at the elbow around 90° minimum to facilitate the press (7). Upon regrasping the bars the gymnast must press quickly downwards to cause the body to rise to support before the body begins to accelerate in the downswing (8). Once the push is complete and the arms are locked out, the shoulders are taken forwards to control the downswing (9).

Note: With good condition the gymnast may eventually take the backward roll into handstand during the phase (positions 6–9 above).

B. Developing the backward roll

    i.   Pushing strength: the gymnast must first develop a powerful press to handstand as shown below.

    ii. Simulating the release and press.

iii. Upper arm swing to the inverted position on the parallel bars to the point of release: this must be practised many times to develop the timing and correct shape, i.e. to position 5 in the diagrams showing the technique in 20.3 A). The coach must support below the bars at the back of the legs (hamstrings) and middle of the back in both the upswing and downswing.

iv. The backward roll: the coach supports from a platform and reaches over and between the bars to support at the thighs and chest as shown below.

20.4 The back uprise

A. The technique

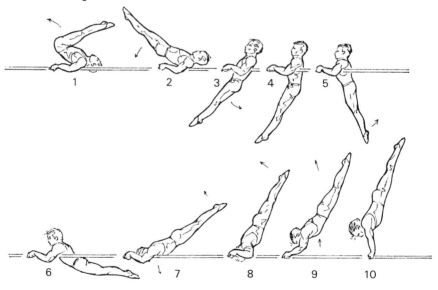

holding the shoulders down, drives the body to the inverted position and begins to suck in the chest (7 and 8). With the hips well above the shoulders and the body entering into the upper quarter of the swing with forward rotation, the gymnast thrusts strongly downwards with the arms to cause the body to rise. The thrust commences at position 8 and can continue with the upswing at 9 and 10 until the arms are straight. The shoulders then move forwards to control the downswing.

Note: With good condition the gymnast will be able to progress the back up into handstand without amending the technique.

B.   Developing the back uprise

i.   Improving the pressing strength.

ii.   *Developing the swing*

Using the technique as described in (A) above, the gymnast, assisted by the coach, swings into position 8 with the shoulders remaining downwards. The coach supports under the bars on the gymnast's thighs and chest in both the upswing and downswing.

iii.   The back uprise is then performed with assistance from above the bar but may still be helpful for a coach or helper, to assist the upswing beneath the bars.

20.5   The underswing cast to upper arm support

A.   The technique

There are two generally accepted techniques used in performing this element, the 'scoop' action and the 'forward swing' method. The scoop action may have more benefits in relation to other elements.

i. *The scoop method*

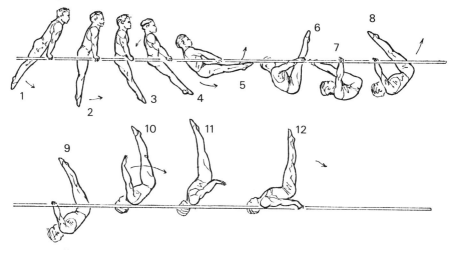

The downswing commences with the shoulders slightly in front of the hands and the body is held straight (1). As the shoulders move backwards to the vertical line the body is dished to cause the feet to lead the swing (2). The hips remain behind the hands and as the feet move in front of the hands the shoulders are forced quickly backwards to increase the swing (3).

The shoulders continue to swing downwards and then continue to fold into a deep pike through positions 4 to 7. At this point the upswing commences with the seat being driven upwards, and the shoulder angle is rapidly removed (8). This action of pulling backwards against the bars is followed by an upward strike of the legs and a further strong pull just prior to release of the hands (9). The body should continue to extend upwards while the arms are swung rapidly forward to regrasp the bars before the downswing commences.

Note: The head is held forward throughout the skill.

Developing the scoop type undershoot

a.   Introduce the swing in piked inverted hang first. Coach supports under the bars on the back of the chest and on the back of the legs.

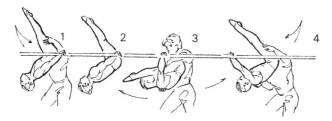

b. At the end of the bars underswing as above and cast away from the bars to land on the platform with the body dished – coach *must* support the landing.

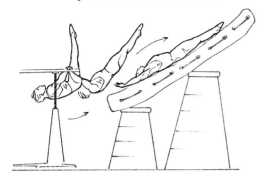

c. Cast to land on padded bars – coach supports as in (a) above.

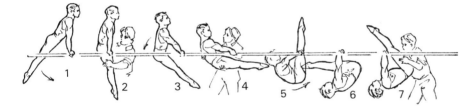

d. Introduce the scoop action as a skill in its own right, the coach supporting under the thighs and under the back of the chest.

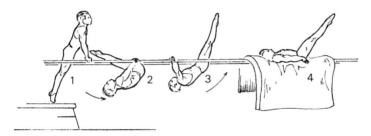

e. The cast from support swing can now be performed with the swing as shown in (d) above and with support to land on padded bars as shown in (c)

f. The complete element is then performed many times to catch in upper arm support but with the coach handling as shown during the learning stages.

ii.   *The forward swing method*

The body swings upwards and forwards into a dish shape at position 1, and the shoulders are momentarily checked and the legs allowed to swing towards a Russian Vee position at 2. As the shoulders begin to drop the seat is drawn backwards behind the hands to increase the swing (3). As the shoulders pass under the bar the seat begins to lead the swing into a similar pattern as described for the scoop type cast.

The teaching of the forward swing type cast will follow a similar sequence to that of the scoop method described earlier.

20.6   **The upstart or kip**

i.   Upstart from support to support

A.   The technique

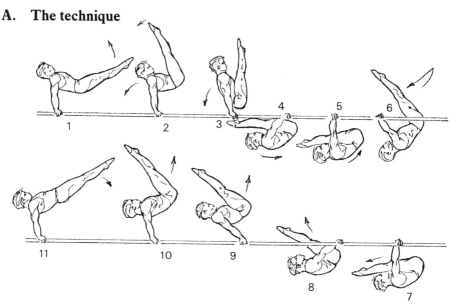

Towards the end of the forward swing (1), the legs are raised towards the chest to form a deep pike (2), and the shoulders drop backwards. The seat is drawn backwards as the shoulders drop, such that the seat leads the swing in a deep pike (3 to 5). The body is slightly extended as the upswing commences to prevent backward rotation (6). The legs again squat downwards to the chest to create a deep pike for the upswing in the opposite direction (7). The gymnast then presses down strongly upon the bars to cause the shoulders to rise (8). At the same time the seat begins to rotate upwards and backwards to move the body into a high vee support (9 to 10). The hips are then extended to commence the downswing. The head should be neutral at all times.

B. Developing the upstart

i.   The upper arm kip.

ii.   Conditioning and awareness skill.

The beat and press is repeated in sets of 10 to develop an understanding of the kip and also improve the pressing strength.

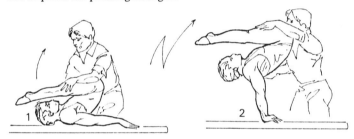

iii.   The upstart is then performed from piked hanging swing beneath the bars. The coach supports beneath the bars, supporting under the chest and at the back of the legs. The gymnast should straddle the legs across the bars in the initial attempts to avoid swinging or collapsing on the downswing. As the gymnast's competence improves the legs may be held together on the downswing but the coach should control the downswing by maintaining the support on the back of the chest and on the back of the legs.

iv.   The gymnast may now perform the complete upstart from support swing as illustrated in (iA), the coach supporting as shown in (iii) above with particular care being taken by the coach to support the gymnast on the downswing after completion of the upstart. The gymnast must not bend the arms at any point during the upstart and must maintain straight arms during the latter aspect of the downswing to resist the powerful forces developed in the downswing.

ii.   The float upstart

A.   The technique

The knees are bent to allow the body to move forwards over the feet (1). The legs are then vigorously straightened to push the hips rearwards and the gymnast presses down on the bars to elevate the body behind the hands (2). This position provides greater potential for downward swing. The body is held in a dished shape until the feet have passed in front of the hands. At this point the body is extended on the upswing and the angle in the shoulders is totally removed (3 and 4). Just prior to the top of the swing the hips are rapidly flexed to cause the body to fold (5). As the downswing commences the body continues to fold into a deep pike (6 and 7). The pike is maintained as the gymnast presses down on the bars to cause the upstart to occur (8). The body is then extended to facilitate the swing in support.

B.   Developing the float upstart

i.   A competent performance of the upstart from support to support as described in 20.5i is an important prerequisite to the learning of the float upstart.

ii.   The front extension and fold into pike should then be taught as follows:

iii.   The gymnast may now attempt the complete float and upstart as shown in the illustration of the technique. The coach will support beneath the bars with the hands supporting at the rear of the chest and behind the legs on the hamstrings. The supporting method and safety precautions are similar to those described for the upstart from support swing (p. 167).

20.7   The basic longswing in hang

The longswing on parallel bars is another swing concept which is essential to good quality bar work. The basic principles of longswing techniques are best introduced at an early stage in a gymnast's training while his weight is low and his relative grip strength quite high.

A.   The technique

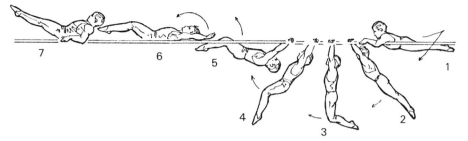

At the commencement of the downswing the body must be fully extended with the angle in the shoulders totally removed (1). The chest will lead the swing slightly in the downswing (2). As the vertical position is approached the legs are bent to clear the floor with the lower legs, but otherwise the body should remain fully extended (3). The legs are now rapidly accelerated so that the knees lead the upswing with approximately a 90° angle being introduced at the hips (4). The angle in the shoulder should also close to allow a rapid upswing of the body (5). As the hips reach the level of the bars the legs and hips are quickly straightened followed by a strong pull backwards on the bars to remove the angle in the shoulders and produce a degree of elevation above the bars (6). At this point the gymnast may release the hands from the bars and regrasp in upper arm hang as shown in position 7. *Or* he may retain the grasp on the bars at position 6, and commence a downswing into hang. The return swing is the reverse of the technique described above with the *introduction of a pull downwards on the bar and a regrasping of the hands when the gymnast approaches the top of the swing at position 1*.

B.   Developing the longswing in hang

i.   Introduce the swing, with a basic technique as described above, on a low horizontal bar of sufficient height to allow the gymnast's legs to clear the floor. This may then be transferred to the parallel bars with the coach supporting in front of and behind the chest as shown:

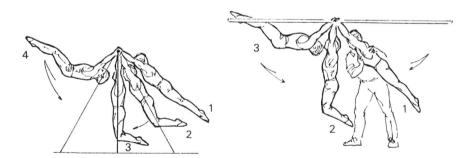

Note: The gymnast must 'press' and 'regrasp' at the top of the swing at position 1.

ii.   From upper arm swing layout into full hanging swing when the body is level with the bars. The coach should support on the front of the chest and front of the thighs during the downswing and then transfer the hand quickly to behind the chest and thighs for the forwards upswing. The hands are again transferred to the front of the chest and thighs for the backwards upswing.

iii.   The gymnast may now attempt, with a similar support as shown in (ii), the full
        longswing from upper arm hang to swing and regrasp in upper arm hang.

If the above technique is taught correctly it can be readily developed at a later stage into a
Moy and longswing to catch in handstand, together with possibilities of turns and various
forms of dismounts.

20.8   The forward roll

A.   The technique

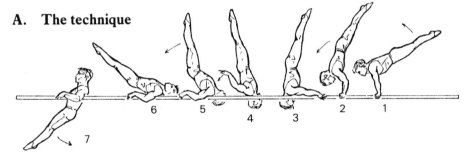

When the hips are above the shoulders in the upswing (1) the arms begin to bend and the
elbows are rotated forwards and outwards (2). The body continues to swing slowly forwards
and the arms lower the shoulders with control onto the bars with the elbows forced
downwards and outwards (3). As the body moves through the vertical line the body is dished
slightly, the head moves forward to enable the gymnast to see his feet, and the arms are
transferred rapidly to regrasp the bar, with *elbows out* (4 and 5). Upon regrasp the gymnast
presses down upon the bars to maintain a high shoulder support position. During the
downswing (6 and 7) the body remains slightly dished in anticipation of an acceleration of
the legs under the bars.

B.   Developing the forward roll

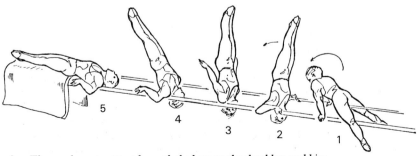

i.   *The coach must support beneath the bars on the shoulders and hips.*

ii.   The gymnast performs the straddle lift to shoulder balance and rolls forward as shown in (i) above but without the mat over the bars. The gymnast swings down with the *coach supporting under the rear of the chest and the back of the thighs, under the bars, to control the swing down to upper arm hang.*

iii.   Introducing the swing but with the mat being slid along the bars to cover the bars as the roll is commenced.

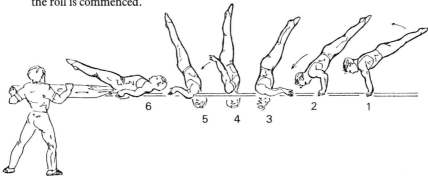

iv.   The complete skill can now be performed from full support swing to upper arm hang swing but with the *coach supporting under the shoulders and at the rear of the thighs to control the swing, and avoid a possible collapse by* the gymnast when in the shoulder balance position.

Note: Shoulder dips, both in upper arm hang and in shoulder balance position, are useful conditioning exercises to develop good shoulder support strength.

20.9   Front somersault (salto) dismount

A.   The technique

To commence the downswing the body is extended in front of the shoulders and the shoulders move forward to a position directly above the hands (1). The body remains dished and is forced forwards and downwards to increase the swing (2). Just prior to the vertical position the legs are accelerated to cause the heels to lead the swing (3). The shoulders now move quickly forwards as the legs continue to cause an arched body shape on the upswing (4). The *shoulders and body are now displaced towards the bar over which the somersault is to travel* and the hips are rapidly elevated when they reach the horizontal position with the

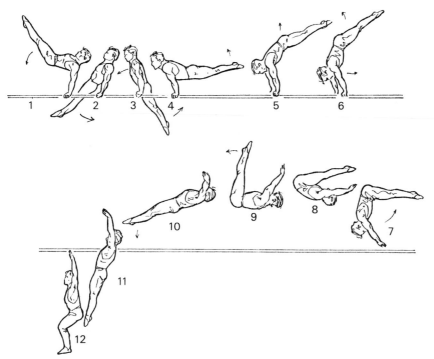

shoulders (5). As the hips continue to lead the swing the gymnast now presses downwards and sideways on the bars to elevate and displace the hips towards one bar (left bar in a left travelling dismount) (6). The shoulders are brought backwards towards the hands and as the trunk approaches a vertical position a final thrust of the arms is exerted against the bars to cause a release and increased elevation (7). The legs are now decelerated and the momentum transferred to the upper body which now folds towards the legs into a deep pike while the arms are taken out to the side (8). As the chest meets the legs the momentum is transferred to the legs and they are snapped downwards in anticipation of the landing (9 and 10). The body is extended and the arms are raised above the head to lengthen the body to reduce rotation prior to landing (10). Landing is completed in a demi plié position (10).

The sideways movement of the body.

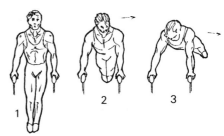

B.   Developing the front salto dismount

i.   The first stage is to develop the basic swing as shown in the illustration of the technique (1 to 6). This action must be practised many times until it can be performed fluently.

ii.   Teaching the sideways hop (see drawing at top of facing page). The direction of travel will be to the gymnast's natural way and will usually be travelling to the left if a gymnast is dominant in a leftward twisting direction.

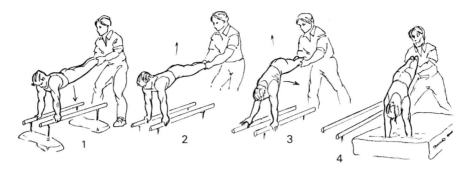

iii.   Understanding the piked salto action.

iv.   The sideways hop from swing should now be performed as shown below.

v.   The front salto dismount onto a platform.

vi.   The complete front salto dismount can now be practised on to a single safety mattress landing surface with the coach supporting under the hips and shoulders as shown in (v) above.

20.10   The backward somersault dismount

A.   The technique

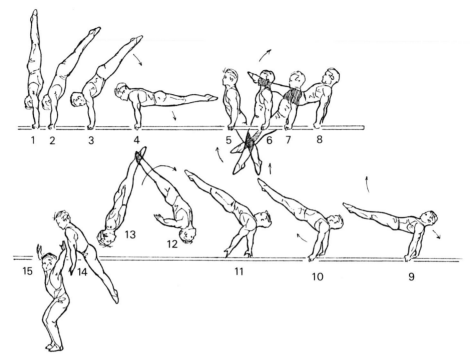

The body should be fully extended in the handstand position (1) prior to the feet being diplaced to cause the downswing to commence (2). The body is held straight (3) until the horizontal position through the shoulders is reached and the hips are then rapidly accelerated to lead the swing (4). The legs then commence the drive through the support position (5) and the feet lead the upswing (6). The shoulders are now displaced backwards and sideways towards the bar over which the gymnast is to travel (7). The feet continue to lead the body into a dished shape while swinging against gravity (8). As the upper body approaches the horizontal position with the shoulders the body is extended and the chest and hips are forced upwards to convert the rotation of the body into elevation (9 and 10). A final thrust from the arms (at 11) releases the bars and adds to the elevation (12). The arms are brought to the side to reduce the inertia and allow greater rotation (13). As the body passes through the inverted vertical position the shoulders are lifted upwards (14) to cause the legs to drop in readiness for the landing (15).

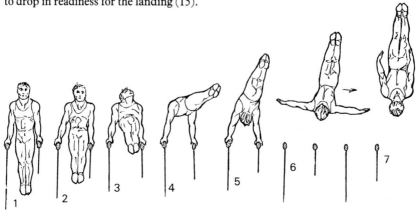

B.   Developing the back somersault dismount

i.   The gymnast must first practise the basic swing technique as described in (a) above (1 to 10), until the pattern is performed fluently.

ii.   An understanding of the skill is introduced on low parallel bars as shown below.

The chest must elevate off the bars and from the inverted position the shoulders are lifted to cause the feet to descend to the landing surface.

iii.   The gymnast may now perform a sideways hop from the front swing to land on the back of the shoulders with the arms extended above the head to break the fall. The landing surface must be level with the height of the bars.

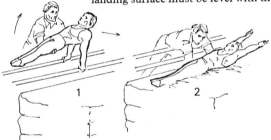

iv.   The back somersault to land on a high platform is introduced as the next skill. The coach must support at the opposite side of the bars to the direction of side travel of the gymnast. The coach should support with one hand in the middle of the shoulders, just below the neck to control the shoulders and with the other hand under the gymnast's buttocks to create elevation and rotation. Remember that the gymnast must also be moved sideways to clear the bars.

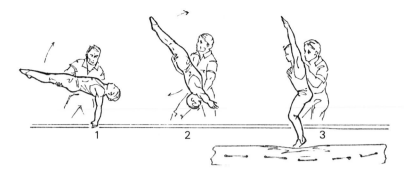

v.   Once the gymnast can perform the dismount safely in the situation shown in (iv), he
may now perform the full skill from the parallel bars onto a safe landing surface. The
coach would support the gymnast as shown above during the initial attempts, until the
gymnast is both competent and confident to perform the skill unaided.

Note: The head should be held forward until the point of release from the bars at which
point the head may be taken into a backwards or neutral position during the flight.

21.0   Horizontal bar exercises

A large number of horizontal bar elements relate closely to elements on other pieces of
apparatus and it is good practice to teach similar skills on varying apparatus at the same
time. Thus more repetitions are performed and the skill will be constantly reinforced in a
variety of situations. Many of the horizontal bar skills can be 'shaped' on floor and developed
on the low bar.

21.1   Types of grasp

The following text will be a useful reminder to both the gymnast and coach with regard to
the type of grasp and the direction of rotation around the bar.

A.   The general rules

i.   The thumbs should always be around the bar and in contact with the index finger when
grasping the horizontal bar.

ii.   The direction of rotation around the bar should *be in the direction of movement of the heel
of the hand*. It should be noted, however, that there are a few exceptions to this rule and
care should be taken to ensure the correct grasp is selected.

B.   Types of grasp

i.   *Overgrasp of the hands*

ii.   *Undergrasp of the hands*

Backward rotation

Forward rotation

   iii.   Mixed grasp: one hand in overgrasp, one in undergrasp.

   iv.   Crossed grasp: the arms are crossed and both hands are in overgrasp.

   v.   Elgrip grasp: the arms are rotated to grasp backwards on the bar, fingers over the bar, thumbs under the bar.

C.   Regrasping the bar

The gymnast should always prepare the hands with an adequate quantity of magnesium carbonate to provide a safe grasp and a grip change or regrasp of the bar should take place during the 'safe zone' (usually at the top) of the swing.

21.2   The drop upstart

A.   The technique (grasp in overgrasp)

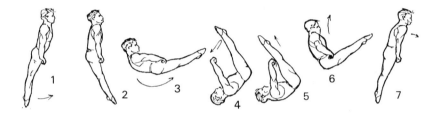

With the body in a slight 'dished' shape (1) the shoulders are displaced backwards to cause backward rotation and the hips are pressed against the bar in the downswing (2 and 3). As the hips pass beneath the bar they are allowed to drift upwards and away from the bar until the hips are level with the bar at (4). The legs then squat quickly to the bar with the ankle and shins almost touching the bar (5). The bar is then pressed down the line of the leg to cause the shoulders to rise above the bars (6).

It should be noted that since the centre of gravity is brought close to the bar the skill is of a rotational nature and *the gymnast must NOT beat the legs away from the bar.*

The bar is continually pressed into the hips until the shoulders are in front of the hands (7). The head should remain forward throughout the skill.

B.   Developing the drop upstart

   i.   The gymnast rehearses the drop and swing as shown in the illustration of the technique in (A) above, positions 1 to 5. The coach should support at the rear of the chest and behind the thighs.

   ii.   An understanding of the pressing action with the arms can be developed using the following skills.

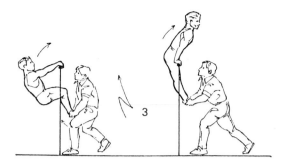

iii.   The upstart is attempted from swing in piked hang position with the coach supporting as shown.

iv.   The complete drop and upstart may now be performed from support returning back to support with the coach assisting as shown in (iii) above.

21.3   The float upstart

A.   The technique (grasp in overgrasp)

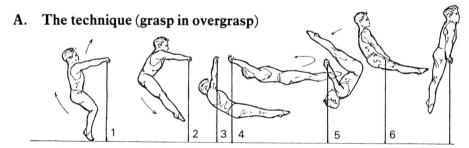

The legs are rapidly straightened to push the hips upwards and backwards behind the bar while the gymnast presses down on the bar to elevate the shoulders (1 and 2). The legs are raised forwards into a 'deep dished' shape as the forward swing commences (2). The body is extended to the height of its swing at 3 to 4, at which point the hips are rapidly flexed to bring the ankles to the bar (5). The bar is then pressed down the line of the legs to bring the hips and the centre of gravity towards the bar (6). Continued pressing down on the bar will cause the shoulders to rise to support above the bar (7).

B.   Developing the front float upstart

i.   A prerequisite to the float upstart is the ability to perform the drop upstart as described in 21.2.

ii.   The float action can be taught as follows:

iii. The gymnast then completes the float upstart commencing with a 'run through' under the bars as shown.

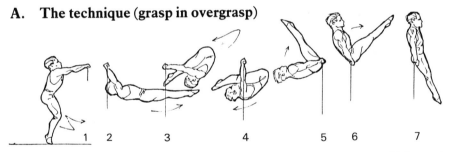

iv.   The complete float upstart can now be practised with the coach assisting as shown in (iii) above.

21.4   Squat legs between hands and uprise to support

A.   The technique (grasp in overgrasp)

The float action is similar to that described for the float upstart in 21.3. At the highest point of the forward swing the hips are rapidly flexed to squat the legs to the chest. The angle between the upper body and arms should remain fully open as the body folds (3). The feet then pass between the hands and the legs continue to squat until the knees are in line with the arms and the body is in a deep pike (4). The gymnast then presses downwards on the bar to cause the shoulders to rise and the body begins to extend as the hips pass above the bar (5). Prior to the shoulders arriving in a vertical position the body is extended to reduce rotation of the body (6) until finally coming to rest above the bar (7).

B.   Developing the squat-in and uprise

i.   The gymnast must first learn the float action as described in 21.3.

ii.   The rhythm and action of the squat and uprise can be learnt as shown.

iii. The uprise action is then rehearsed from a swing in piked hang position. The coach should support under the back of the chest and hamstrings during the uprise and then ensure that over-rotation does not occur when the gymnast is in support above the bar. This may be done by the coach replacing the hand supporting the back of the legs as shown.

iv. The gymnast must learn to squat the feet between the hands by (a) running under the bar, float and squat the legs between the hands, (b) then from a float, squat the legs between the hands.

v. When the float and squat-in has been effectively mastered the gymnast may practise the complete element float squat-in and uprise to support, with the coach assisting as shown and described in (iii) above.

21.5 The reverse or back upstart

A. The technique (grasp in overgrasp)

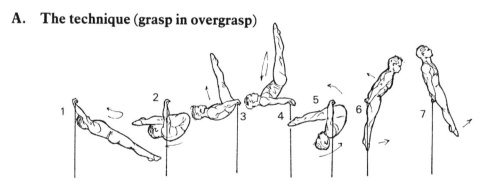

The float and squat-in with the legs (1 to 3) is similar to the technique described in 21.04 but during the upswing the gymnast presses the bar downwards, causing the shoulders to rise (4). The body is also extended upwards at this point to give maximum potential for the following downswing. The body is then folded into a deep pike position beneath the bar at 5. To reduce the retardation effect of the gravitational force during the upswing the gymnast must quickly and strongly press downwards on the bar to *draw the seat towards the bar*. At

the same time the legs are checked and the momentum transferred to the upper body to
cause the shoulders to rise at 6. The wrists are then extended to allow a regrasp of the hands
as the shoulders rise above the bar.

B.   Developing the reverse or back upstart

i.   A prerequisite to learning this skill is the performance of the squat-in and uprise as
     described in 21.04.

ii.   The reverse upstart action is then taught from a piked hang position beneath the bar.

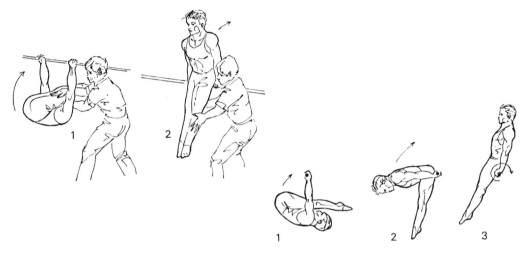

The coach firmly holds the legs beneath the bar (1) and the gymnast can then act
against the legs to make the reverse upstart action and regrasp of the bar. The coach
must also press the gymnast's seat towards the bar by lifting upwards with the
gymnast's legs (2).

iii.   The action of squatting in with the legs and elevation of the body above the bar on the
      rearward swing is then developed on the floor.

Emphasis should be placed upon the open shoulder angle during the squat at 1 to 2 and
the action of pressing downwards with the hands on the bar to elevate the body at 4.
The seat is then drawn under the bar at 5.

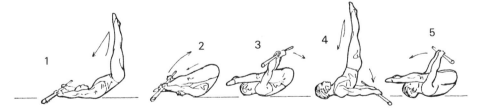

iv.   The sequence shown in (iii) above is then practised upon the low bar with the coach
     supporting at the rear of the bar, upon the gymnast's chest and back. Care should be
     taken not to allow the hips to move beyond the vertical line through the shoulders in the
     position shown. However, the gymnast should endeavour to press down on the bar to
     raise the shoulders level with the bar to give maximum potential for the forthcoming
     downward swing.

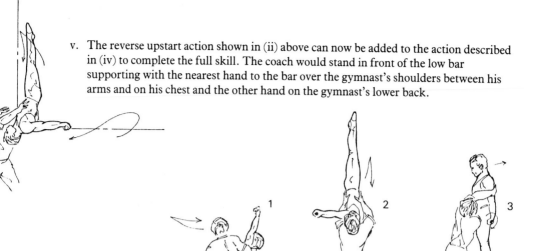

v. The reverse upstart action shown in (ii) above can now be added to the action described in (iv) to complete the full skill. The coach would stand in front of the low bar supporting with the nearest hand to the bar over the gymnast's shoulders between his arms and on his chest and the other hand on the gymnast's lower back.

1.6   Forward hip circle

A.   The technique (grasp in overgrasp)

(An exception to the general rule regarding type of grasp and direction of rotation)

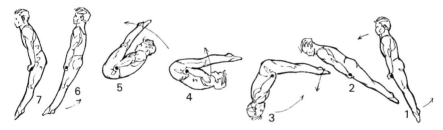

The gymnast commences from support in overgrasp on the bar. The heels are lifted and the tensioned straight body is tilted forward to commence the forward rotation with a straight body (1). As the body approaches the horizontal position the feet are retarded and as the upper body is quickly 'piked' around the bar to take the chest towards the legs, the hands are rapidly regrasped forwards under the bar (2 to 4). With the body in a deep fold, the body continues to rotate forwards around the bar to position 5, at which point the body begins to extend to slow down the rotation and the gymnast presses the bar into the hips to complete the element in full support (6 and 7).

B.   Developing the forward hip circle

i. With the coach holding the gymnast's legs and under the chest the gymnast is lowered from front support into the horizontal position shown in (2) above. The coach will hold the legs in the horizontal position and with the other hand placed behind the back of the gymnast, the gymnast is encouraged to regrasp around the bar as he folds the chest to the legs (3 and 4 above).

ii. With the gymnast in a deep piked fold over the bar, the coach, supporting on the back of the legs and rear of the chest, rocks the gymnast and then assists the upward circle to support.

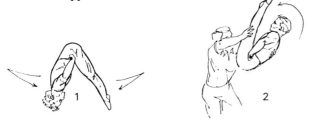

iii. With the coach standing in front of the bar, supporting with the nearest hand under the bar to lift the gymnast's legs, and the other hand on the upper back, the full skill can now be attempted. The coach assists in stopping the legs and rapidly folding the body. As the gymnast's chest passes beneath the bar the hand is removed from the legs and is quickly replaced on the gymnast's upper back to assist the upward circle. The first hand is removed from the gymnast's back and catches the gymnast's legs as they circle over the bar, to bring the gymnast safely to rest in support.

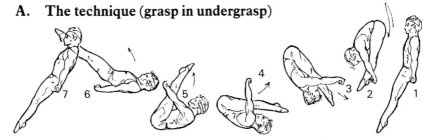

21.7 Forward seat circle

A. The technique (grasp in undergrasp)

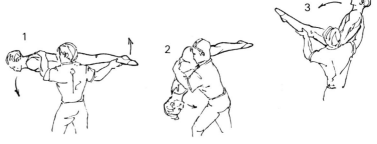

Commencing from a seated back support position on the bar with the hands in undergrasp (1) the gymnast elevates the centre of gravity as high as possible above the bar. This is achieved by lifting the seat upwards above the shoulders (2). The gymnast then moves the thighs forwards into the chest to move the centre of gravity away from the bar and squats the legs downwards between the arms (3). The body should be in a deep fold directly beneath the bar to obtain maximum swing (4). During the upswing the gymnast presses downwards on the bar to cause the shoulders to rise, but the body is held in a pike position (5) until the shoulders approach the horizontal position. The body is extended to slow down the rotation and the gymnast continues to press downwards upon the bar (6). As the shoulders move above the bar the hands are shifted to regrasp forwards to aid in the blocking of the shoulders as the body comes to rest above the bar (7).

B. Developing the forward seat circle

i.   An understanding of the pressing action on the bar can be created by use of the following skill.

ii. Commencing in piked hang position beneath the bar, hands in undergrasp, the gymnast is assisted in developing a basic swing. Remember to regrasp at the top of each backward swing (at the top of the swing in which the seat is leading). With the coach supporting at the hamstring and the centre of the gymnast's back, the gymnast performs the uprise to sit on the bar. Over-rotation over the bar can be avoided if the coach quickly transfers his hand from the legs, under the bar and again supports at the lower legs.

iii. With the gymnast seated upon the bar, the coach, supporting the gymnast at the rear of the chest and at the rear of the lower leg, assists the gymnast, elevating the seat upwards and away from the bar. The downwards swing into piked hang can now be rehearsed.

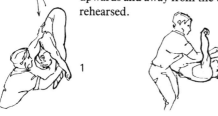

iv. With the downward swing and the uprise aspects now mastered the gymnast may now combine them to perform the complete forward seat circle. The coach, standing at the rear of the bar, supports the gymnast at the lower and upper back during the underswing and uprise.

21.8 Straddle sole circle backwards

A. The technique (grasp in overgrasp)

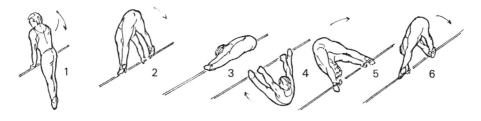

The element commences with a hip beat action (1), with the shoulders moving in front of the bar to enable the hips to be raised quickly above the bar at (2) with the feet placed just outside the hands to ensure that the centre of gravity is maintained away from the bar. The gymnast pushes downwards on the bar through the arms and extends the ankles to create the downswing (3). Throughout the swing the ankles must be fully extended to maintain the contact with the feet on the bar, particularly as the body passes beneath the bar at (4). During the upswing the gymnast pulls down strongly on the bar to cause the shoulders to rise (5). As the gymnast aproaches the vertical position he must make a rapid wrist change to regrasp the hands to permit the shoulders to rise to support.

B.   Developing the straddle sole circle backwards

i.   The coach assists at the rear of the bar, supporting the gymnast at the rear of the legs as shown. The coach then lowers the gymnast through to the straddle hang position. A second coach may support in front of the bar to prevent a forward rotation over the bar.

ii.   With two coaches supporting as shown in (1) above, the gymnast is allowed gently to swing through straddle support and the coach in front of the bar assists at the shoulders to raise the gymnast through the upswing to support on the bar.

iii.   The complete element can now be performed with the coach supporting from the front of the bar, assisting at the ankle and upper arm. It is important for the coach to note that the hand supporting on the upper arm must reach *under* the bar before making contact with the gymnast's arm.

21.9   Backward hip circle to handstand

A.   The technique (grasp in overgrasp)

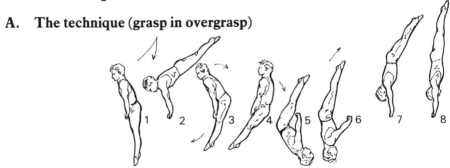

From the front support position the gymnast performs a hip beat layaway to a high support position (1 and 2). The body is then 'dished' by bringing the thighs to the bar with the bar placed just above the knees (3). The shoulders are then quickly forced backwards to increase the momentum of the downswing (4). The bar is pressed into the thighs until the shoulders are directly beneath the bar (5), at which point the gymnast begins to open out the shoulder angle by drawing the bar strongly backwards (6). As the gymnast approaches the handstand a rapid wrist change and regrasp is introduced (7), and the gymnast presses the angle fully out of the shoulders (8). The body must remain dished, and the head should be held in a neutral position throughout the exercise.

B. The development of the backward hip circle to handstand

i.   The performance of a straight arm backward roll to handstand on floor is a particularly good related skill. It is important to emphasise the need to retain the tensioned dish shape, particularly during the arm pressing phase. The gymnast should turn the hands inwards to reduce the stress on the wrists. The coach should support around the hip region to help maintain the correct body shape.

ii. With the gymnast in the inverted position, with thighs against the bar, the two coaches carry the gymnast through the upward swing phase to handstand. Coach B supports in front of the bar and assists under the shoulders, while coach A supports on the legs from a position above the bar.

iii. The hip circle may now be commenced from a static support position above the bar with two coaches assisting as shown in 2 above. With the dished position created by the gymnast, the shoulders are forced backwards to initiate the circle and the circle to handstand is completed as shown above.

iv. With the coaches assisting as described above, the gymnast performs the full skill from a hip beat layaway.

v.   As the gymnast's proficiency improves one coach can handle the supporting *either* from position 1 or 2 as shown in (ii) above *or* by supporting from in front of the bar with the assistance being provided at the front and rear of the chest from beneath the bar and into handstand as shown below.

vi. The skill may be developed with the hips remaining clear of the bar.

Note: The following exercises are of great help in improving both understanding and strength.

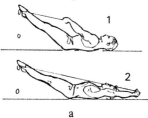

a

b

21.10 Back uprise

A. The technique
(grasp in overgrasp)

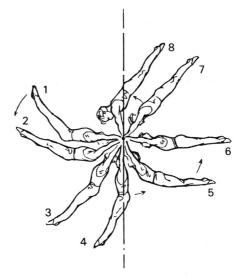

The body should be fully extended to develop maximum momentum during downswing from 1 to 2. A slight dish is introduced just before passing beneath the bar (3) and the dish is maintained until the hips have passed under the bar (4). The reaction from the dish is to accelerate the legs ahead of the body to create an arched body shape in which the heels lead the upswing (5). The shoulders and head are held down during the upswing and as the hips rise above the line of the bar the gymnast introduces a strong downward pressing action from the arms against the bar (6). The body continues to rise as the pressing action, and closing action of the angle between the arms and shoulders, cause the shoulders to move upwards and towards the bar (7). The element is completed with the shoulders marginally in front of the bar and the hips above the line of the shoulders (8).

As the gymnast's competence and strength improves he may eventually perform this element towards the handstand position above the bar.

Note: When teaching this element to inexperienced gymnasts good support must be provided as the gymnast passes under the bar from 3 to 6 in the above illustration.

B. Developing the back uprise

    i.   Developing the strength and awareness for the pressing phase.

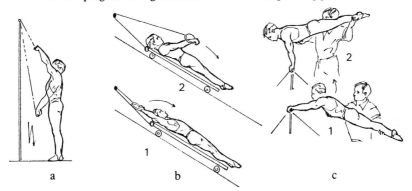

   a   b   c

    ii.   The layout and under bar swing (trolley swing) is then introduced as follows. From a gentle backswing the gymnast performs a chin-up action and follows this with a rapid

piking action at the hips. As the hips circle forwards and upwards in front of the bar
the gymnast presses backwards upon the bar to cause the arms to straighten and the
body extends away from the bar. The coach should support under the shoulders and
behind the upper legs during this phase. As the gymnast descends, the coach should
reach through to make early contact with one hand around the upper arm and the
other hand under the front of the thighs of the gymnast.

The gymnast should initially rehearse the swing up the back – to regrasp the hands
and swing down again.

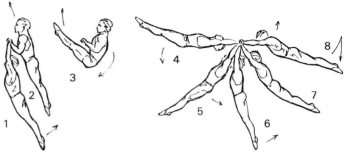

iii. The back uprise may now be added to the basic swing described in (ii) above. The
      coach must provide good assistance during the swing under the bar and during the
      back uprise to support. Support at the front of the thighs and on the upper arm or
      under the chest.

iv.   When the gymnast can competently perform the back uprise from the layout swing it is
      possible to progress to back uprise commencing from support above the bar as shown
      below. This will increase the degree of swing and should allow a higher finishing point
      during the back uprise. The coach must provide good support as previously described
      in (iii) above, and it should be remembered that this skill should only be introduced to
      the more competent gymnast.

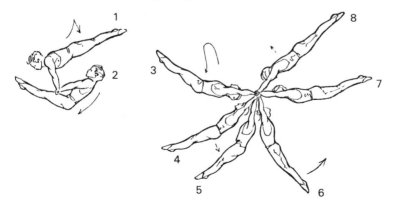

Note: The gymnast should retain a good hand grasp with the hands in plantar extension
during the phase changing from upswing to downswing (2 to 3).

21.11 Backward giant swing (longswing)

The giant swing, both backwards and forwards, is the foundation upon which the majority of horizontal bar skills are based. A thorough understanding of the mechanical principles as described in Section 9.3 f(i), together with good body tension conditioning, will greatly enhance the learning and teaching of the giant swings.

A. The technique (grasp in overgrasp)

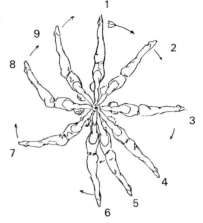

In the handstand position (1) the gymnast extends the body fully to gain maximum potential. A slight dish is introduced into the body to initiate the swing and this tensioned, extended body shape is held throughout the downswing (2, 3 and 4). At (5) the hips are relaxed to permit the hips to lead the swing under the bar (6). This hollow shape is introduced to produce an action, the reaction of which is to assist the rapid acceleration of the legs into the upswing. Once the gymnast has passed beneath the bar an angle is introduced into the shoulders and into the hips to help maintain the momentum of the upswing (7). The dished shape and shoulder angle is maintained through (8) until the force due to the bend of the bar is returned to the body. This occurs just before the handstand position and at this point the shoulder angle is rapidly removed and a 'wrist change' introduced to give a regrasp of the hands (9). The dished body shape is still maintained so that the feet lead the swing to the handstand position where the body is again fully extended to commence the next downswing.

It will be helpful for the coach and gymnast to remember that when swinging down with gravity the body should be extended for maximum swing (from 1 to 6) and when swinging upwards against the effects of gravity the body should be shortened (i.e. closing of the hip and shoulder angle from 6 to 1) to maintain momentum.

B. Developing the backward giant swing

An important prerequisite to the performance of a giant swing is the ability to maintain good mid-body tension as described in Section 21.6. The following sequence of skills will be helpful progressions.

    i.   The gymnast to maintain a 'dished' shape throughout.

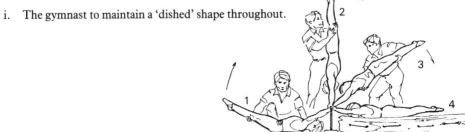

ii.   Teach the basic swing in hang – dish – relax hips – kick.

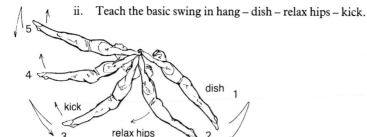

On the return backswing to position (1) the gymnast must pull on the bar and regrasp the bar before re-commencing the downswing. *Do not* permit the gymnast to extend the body at the top of the forward swing (5), but encourage the retention of the dished shape at this point. The coach should support at the upper arm and hips throughout the swing.

To dismount the gymnast should, during the initial learning stages, push off the bar to land just after the body has commenced the downswing from position (1).

iii.   *Layaway and swing down*

Coach A assists in the layaway to handstand and ensures that the dished shape is held during the downswing; coach B reaches to make contact with the gymnast on the chest and thighs and controls the gymnast during the downswing.

iv.   *Overbalance and regrasp*

There will undoubtedly be an occasion when the gymnast will overbalance when laying up to handstand or when failing to reach handstand during a giant swing. A useful safety outlet is for the gymnast to rehearse a reverse fall and regrasp of the hands, still in overgrasp, during the reverse swing down.

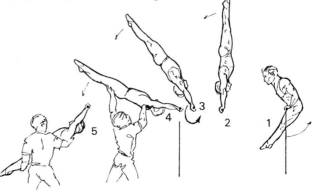

v.   *The overbar swing*

This exercise is useful in providing awareness during the phase involving the upward swing and swing across the bar. The gymnast should be encouraged to maintain a deep dish from the float swing and throughout the skill. Straight arms should also be maintained and the strong wrist change for regrasp of the hands should be introduced just before handstand.

The gymnast should dismount by pushing off to land as the body commences a downswing from position (1).

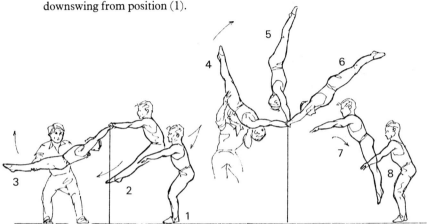

vi.   *Giant swing on a ¾ height bar*

The gymnast performs the giant swing from a layaway on a ¾ height bar. Coach A, standing at just above shoulder height with the bar, shapes the gymnast in the handstand position prior to the downswing. He then reaches under the bar with his nearest hand to grasp the gymnast's upper arm. During the upswing coach A assists under the upper arm and under the thighs to guide the gymnast across the bar. A second coach (B) may be used on the opposite side in a similar manner to coach A *or* may support under the hips and chest during the swing phase beneath the bars.

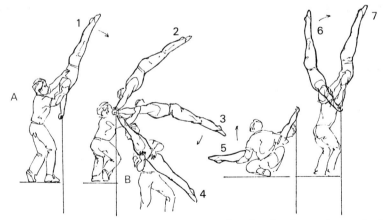

vii.   The gymnast may now progress to performing the giant swing on the full height horizontal bar with the coach or coaches assisting as described in (vi) previously. The gymnast may be permitted to bend his legs during the upswing to maintain the momentum during the initial attempts.

C. Safety in teaching the backward giant swing

i. Good body tension should be maintained throughout the element with the exception of the relaxation phase beneath the bar.

ii. The gymnast will possess maximum momentum as he passes under the bar and it is at this point where the gymnast is most likely to require support to avoid loss of grasp.

iii. Should the gymnast fail to reach handstand during the giant swing, he will require good support on the downswing as he will be swinging in incorrect grasp.

iv. The following training aids will be invaluable in the teaching of the giant swings.

   i. *The safety harness*

The belt is placed over the bar and the harness attached around the gymnast's waist. Should the gymnast lose his grasp at the bottom of the swing the belt will prevent him departing from the bar.

   ii. *Loops and leather sleeves*

The leather sleeves are placed around a *polished* bar and the loops are draped over the bar. The hands are placed through the loops with the palms facing downwards and fingers pointing away from the body. The hands are then turned inwards, then lift the hands to grasp the bar with the loops outside the hands.

The loops will offer greater confidence in the grip on the bar while the leather sleeves which rotate around the bar will reduce the friction between the hands and the bar.

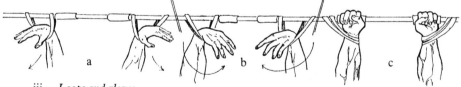

   iii. *Loops and gloves*

The loops and gloves are used in a similar manner to the loops and sleeves and should only be used with a *highly polished bar* to avoid the possibility of the loops locking on the bar. Chalk should not be used with loops and gloves.

The gymnast should be allowed a suitable period of time to become familiar and confident with the use of the gloves and loops by simply swinging in basic hang.

Once confident in the use of the gloves the gymnast will find their use invaluable in the learning of a number of gymnastic skills. They will permit many repetitions without risk of tearing the hands.

21.12   The forward giant swing (grasp in undergrasp)

The same mechanical principles can be applied to the understanding of the forward giant swing as were discussed for the backward giant swing in Section 9.3f(i). The forward giant swing may also be taught with the use of loops and gloves similar to that described earlier but with different looping arrangement (see p. 196).

A.   The technique

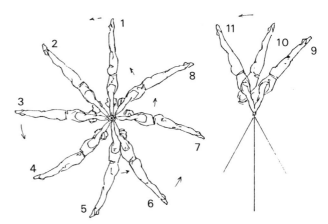

The body should be fully extended in the handstand position (1) to give maximum potential for swing. During the downswing the body should be straight and tensioned (2 and 3) until position (4), where a slight dish may be introduced into the body to cause the hips to lead in the swing. As the body passes through the vertical line (5) the hips are relaxed and the legs are accelerated to lead the initial part of the upswing (6). This body attitude is altered into a dished shape and an angle is introduced into the shoulders by the gymnast pressing downwards upon the bar (7). The gymnast should continue to press downwards on the bar and maintain a dished shape through positions 8, 9 and 10. This will ensure that the body is effectively shortened to maintain the upward momentum and that the shoulders will lead the swing. The shoulders are drawn slightly over the bar (at 10) and the wrists are rotated forwards to regrasp with the hands. The gymnast then presses against the bar to cause the shoulder angle to open and the body to extend in preparation for the next downswing (11).

Note: The smaller the shoulder angle as the body passes over the bar, the faster the body will travel across the bar – and vice versa. Hence, to produce a 'wind-up' giant for forward dismounts the shoulder angle is retained over the bar but where a turn around the longitudinal axis is to be executed the angle in the shoulders is removed just prior to the handstand position.

B.   Developing the forward giant swing

Note: The grasp is in undergrasp.

i.   *The conditioning*

a   Hold for 30 secs   b   Repeat 10 times   c   Repeat 10 times

ii. *Shaping the overswing*

The coach assists at the gymnast's hips to help create the desired dished shape which is then maintained until lying on the safety mattress.

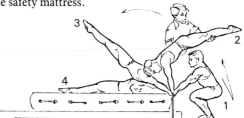

iii. *Awareness in the overswing*

Emphasise the drawing of the shoulders across the bar by pressing downwards on the bar.

iv. *Layaway to handstand*

v. *The shortened giant swing*

Coach A assists the gymnast under the chest and thighs from the underswing to the handstand position (4). Coach B supports behind the gymnast's chest and thighs on the downswing.

vi.   *The forward giant swing on the ¾ height bar*

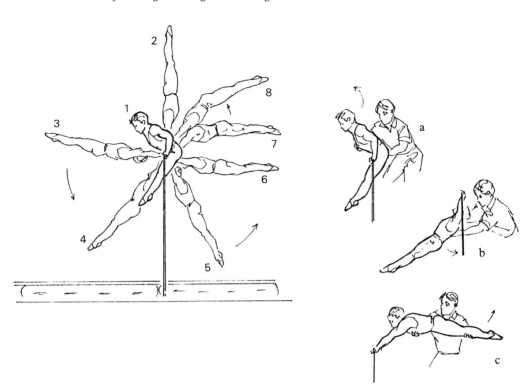

The gymnast performs the forward giant swing at a height just sufficient for him to clear the safety mats. The coach will support initially to assist in the cast or lay up to handstand as shown in (a). Once the gymnast commences the downswing the coach transfers his support, reaching under the bar with his nearest hand to grasp the gymnast's upper arm (b) prior to the gymnast passing under the bar, and then places his second hand under the gymnast's thighs. On the upswing the coach must provide good support at the shoulders and thighs to create the correct shape and reduce the tendency of the gymnast to lose the grasp on the bar as he passes under the bar (c). To dismount, the gymnast should press against the bar at (7) to stop the swing and then push off to land.

vii.   *The complete forward giant swing*

This may now be attempted on the full height of the bar with similar support being provided as described in (vi) above. A second coach may provide similar assistance at the other side of the gymnast or he may assist from the floor, supporting at the chest and thighs as the gymnast passes beneath the bar.

C.   Safety in teaching the forward giant swing

i.   The point of highest risk is when the gymnast is passing beneath the bar and the coach must be alert to provide good support at this point during the learning stages.

ii.   A dished body shape should be a dominant feature in the perfomance and an arching of the back (hollowing) during the swing across the bar should be discouraged.

iii.   The safety harness looped over the bar or loops and gloves (sleeve) may be usefully employed throughout the teaching of the forward giant swing. However, a polished bar must be used in conjunction with the gloves and loops and the hand grasp should be established as follows:

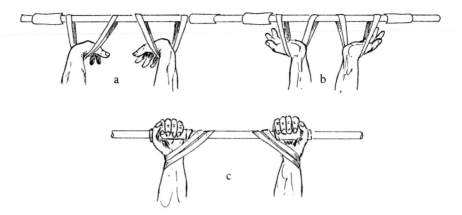

a.   Reach to the far side of the bar and place the hands through the loops, palms down.

b.   Rotate the hands outwards, with the palms up.

c.   Grasp the sleeves or the bar if using gloves with the loops inside the hands.

22.0 Choice of apparatus

The specifications for Olympic Gymnastics apparatus (see section 22.2) are designed to suit the needs of the top-class performer and as such may not always lend themselves readily to the training of young gymnasts.

It is therefore necessary to select the apparatus to suit the size and level of the performer to ensure a safe and effective development. Junior apparatus is available but this can be expensive and it may be a better compromise to purchase or acquire equipment which can be readily adapted to suit a variety of needs.

22.1 Training aids

The following items of equipment and training aids will be useful additions to a training facility.

a. Tumble track panels – i.e. recoil tumbling boards with firm carpeted floor covering of the polyethylene type or similar.

b. Mushroom side horse trainer; bucket trainer and floor level side horse with a wide range of adjustment on the handles.

c. Adjustable height rings, and pulley and harness rings.

d. Vaulting buck with good range on height adjustment. Padding cover for vaulting horse.

e. Swan neck adaptors to permit narrow spacing or bars for primary gymnasts – floor level parallel bars and bars located inside the foam landing pit.

f. Various levels of horizontal bar and a separate polished bar for working in loops and gloves.

g. Trampolines, trampettes and mini tramps are ideal for skill learning, spatial awareness, and as a base for a landing module.

h. Overhead harness rigs for use on tumble, rings, vault, parallel bars, horizontal bar and rebound situations (i.e. trampoline).

i. Ring trolley trainer – essential to the development of strength generally and to the understanding of ring skills.

There are many training aids and new ideas are being developed daily: the BAGA Technical Department will be pleased to advise on choice or new developments.

22.2   Fédération Internationale Gymnastique (F.I.G.) apparatus specifications

The following details will be useful when designing a gymnasium layout or setting up the apparatus for a competition.

Floor exercise
12m square area, carpet covered, with a 1m surround.

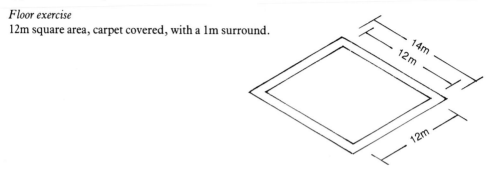

Pommel or side horse

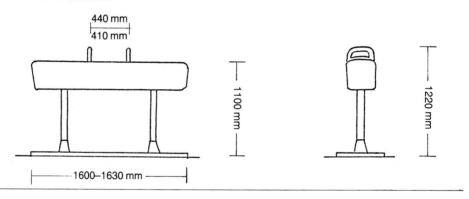

Rings

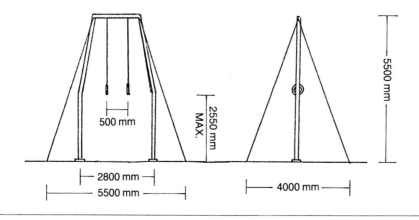

Parallel bars

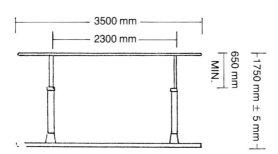
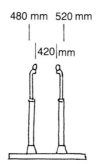

Horizontal bar

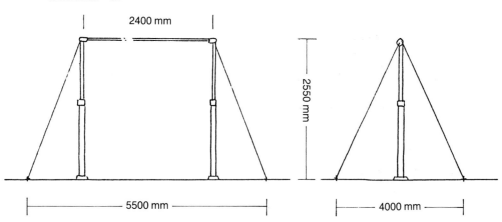

Vault
Horse length: 1600–1630 mm; height 1350 mm; run-up 25 m

23.0 Select bibliography

John Atkinson, ESTEC Coaching Pamphlets (ESGA, 1976)

Edward L. Fox, *Sports Physiology* (Saunders College Publishing, 1979)

J. Fox, *Sports* (ESGA, 1976)

James J. Hay, *Biomechanics of Sports Techniques* (Prentice-Hall Inc., 1973)

Akimoto Kineko, *Olympic Gymnastics*

David R. Lamb, *Physiology of Exercise* (Collier Macmillan, 1984)

Trevor Low (ed.), *Grasp* magazine

National Coaching Foundation, *Introductory Study Packs* and *Coaching Handbooks*

Tony Smith, *Gymnastics – Mechanical Understanding* (Hodder & Stoughton, 1982)

St John's Ambulance Association and Brigade, *First Aid* (Hills & Lacy Ltd)

Nanzi Jingji Ticao and Tupian Xuan, *Chinese Coaching Manual* (1983)

USSR Gymnastic Coaching Booklets (1984)

Eugene Wettstone, *Gymnastic Safety Manual* (US Gymnastic Safety Association, Pennsylvania State University Press, 1979)

Rolf Wirhed, *Athletic Ability and Anatomy of Motion* (Wolfe Medical Publications, 1984)